MAKE DO AND MEND

KEEPING FAMILY AND HOME AFLOAT ON WAR RATIONS

REPRODUCTIONS OF OFFICIAL SECOND WORLD WAR INSTRUCTION LEAFLETS

FOREWORD BY JILL NORMAN

First published in Great Britain in 2007 by
Michael O'Mara Books Limited
9 Lion Yard
Tremadoc Road
London SW4 7NQ

A CIP catalogue record for this book is available from the British Library

ISBN 978-1-84317-265-9

3 5 7 9 10 8 6 4

Designed by Design 23

Printed and bound in Great Britain by
Butler Tanner & Dennis Ltd

Many thanks to Stephen Jones and the staff at the National Archives in Kew
from whose archives the leaflets reproduced in this book were sourced.

CONTENTS

FOREWORD

Food rationing is probably the first thing that comes to mind when the privations of the Second World War are mentioned, but many other taken-for-granted items of daily life were also rationed or in short supply. Recycling, more popular in today's 'green' society than at any time since the years of wartime austerity, was the order of the day in the forties, with paper, old pots and pans and all manner of scrap salvaged to help the war effort.

Fuel to heat your home or for your car or motorcycle was strictly rationed. Coal was needed for industries manufacturing for the war effort, and keeping the military mobile required vast amounts of fuel which became a precious resource as U-boat activity decimated supplies. Petrol was rationed from the beginning of the war in September 1939. Small allowances were granted for private cars and motorcycles; ration books giving the registration number of the vehicle had to be produced at garages. Even these meagre allowances were stopped altogether in 1942, and only people who were 'essential' car users continued to receive ration coupons. In those days far fewer people drove cars, so the lack of petrol affected a relatively small percentage of the population.

The rationing of fuel for the home, with most houses heated by coal fires, had a far more direct effect on the vast majority of ordinary people. Saving fuel was vital to the war effort. Power stations needed coal to supply electricity to factories; many factories themselves needed coal or oil to run their machinery and the whole rail network would have ground to a halt without coal for the steam trains.

Domestic fuel was allocated according to the size of the house and the region where it was located, while everyone was also allocated a personal allowance. The year from July 1942 to June 1943 was called the year of the

THE BATTLE FOR FUEL

Here are your Battle Orders

Every citizen—particularly every housewife—is now in the front line in the vital Battle for Fuel. Everything possible must be done to save fuel. Here, in handy form, you will find a number of hints and suggestions on how best to make day to day savings in your home. Follow these closely and see that the other people in the house do so too. Small economies in many directions soon add up to a really worth-while saving.

1 Fuel Unit Equals
½ Cwt of Coal or Coke or
500 Cubic Feet of Gas
or 50 Units of Electricity
or 1 Gallon of Paraffin

★ Remember, THE FUEL YEAR dates from July 1st 1942 until June 30th 1943. By its terms you mark out on the chart on the back page you can work out the number of Fuel Units you are allowed. Later on keep to dividing them up among the various types of fuel you use. Some of your allowance is used up already and there is cold weather ahead—so go carefully now.

'Battle for Fuel' by the Ministry of Fuel and Power. People were asked to be especially careful in their fuel use, to use large anthracite or coke in boilers and fires, and were shown how to make briquettes of coal dust and sawdust or cement, so that none of the ration was wasted. The need to use fuel sparingly went on throughout the war and beyond, with everyone encouraged to support Britain's economic recovery by saving power that was needed by our industries.

During the war it was essential to maintain a high output of coal, and in 1941 the government decided that the men compulsorily bound to work in the coalmines should have the same welfare facilities as factory workers. Canteens were provided at the pithead, serving snacks during the shifts and a proper meal at the end. For a brief period there was even an experiment in feeding miners underground because it was argued that a full meal in the middle of the shift gave a higher output than a similar meal taken at the end. However, it was too hot and dusty to eat underground, and the idea was abandoned in favour of the pithead canteen.

Having dripping taps mended, washing up in a bowl rather than the sink, taking shallow baths and lagging the hot water tank were some of the ways to economize on fuel suggested in guidelines from the government. Food writers and writers of 'Ministry' leaflets dealt comprehensively with conserving fuel in the kitchen.

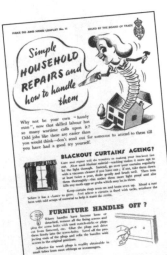

Mrs Arthur Webb,[1] cookery writer on *Farmer's Weekly*, advocated using a pressure cooker or a three-tiered steamer to provide a whole meal; vegetables, meat, puddings, and even a cake could be cooked in a steamer. The cake had to be covered in a double thickness of greaseproof paper, tied securely, and steamed for one hour per pound of mixture. To brown the cake a spoonful of sugar mixed with a little milk was brushed over the top and it was put in the oven briefly, or it could be covered with a simple icing. A make-do steamer could be created out of a large pan filled with enough water to come half way up the sides of three or four earthenware jars. Pot-roasting and casserole cooking were recommended as highly efficient methods; a close-fitting lid and slow cooking preserved heat and used less fuel. The oven was only to be used if several items were to be cooked at the same time.

A multitude of practical tips helped readers minimize the amount of fuel they used. The heat of a gas ring could be extended to more than one pan by putting a baking sheet over it, so that the metal became hot over a wide surface. With a gas cooker it was more economical to fry than to grill; the reverse was true with an electric cooker. Electric and gas ovens would retain heat after being switched off, so milk puddings and other dishes could be finished in the oven after it had been turned off. Electric kettles use only half the current of a boiling plate, so it was better to use a kettle to boil water, and only to put in the amount of water needed. Cookery writers also gave instructions to make a hay box, a large wooden box padded with hay or balls of newspaper, in which pans of food, brought to the boil on the stove, could be left to 'cook' for several hours.

In the diary she kept for the Mass Observation project,[2] Nella Last often mentioned that she cooked a meal by the fire rather than on the stove in order to save fuel. She also wrote of abuses of fuel rationing in her home town, Barrow-in-Furness. Many households bought their coal from the Co-op and women who were unscrupulous placed orders at different branches of the Co-op, so receiving more than their share. The practice came to light when only half-rations for everybody had been delivered to the yard, and many people had to make-do with slag and briquettes.

In the last half-century we have come to take the availability of all types of fuel for granted; we have central heating in our homes, we use washing machines and spin dryers, cookers, refrigerators, radios, televisions and computers. We drive everywhere. We waste appalling amounts of foodstuffs and all kinds of other materials, until fairly recently without reckoning the cost too carefully. Now, with more awareness of carbon emissions, green issues and the changed geo-political environment, we are belatedly realizing that some far-reaching measures are needed. While many of the proposals to save fuel made so urgently in these leaflets are not relevant today, there are lessons to learn. The global urgency to act is just as necessary as was the wartime effort.

Curbs on clothing were just as severe as curbs on the use of fuel. Clothing rationing began in June 1941 and coupon books were issued to every man, woman and child. Each person was allowed a maximum of sixty-six coupons per year, the equivalent of one new outfit a year. Children were allocated ten extra coupons a year and children's clothes had lower coupon values than adults'. The allowance was later cut to forty-eight coupons, then thirty-six and eventually twenty. Clothing rationing went on until 1949. There were special coupons for baby clothes, and families who were bombed out could receive coupons for up to two years' clothing, assuming they could afford to buy the clothes. If not, they could get second-hand clothes from the WVS (Women's Voluntary Service) centres.

The table in *The Clothing Coupon Quiz* (page 69) shows how many coupons were needed for different garments. Knitting wool and cloth for suiting and dressmaking were rationed; blackout material for windows was not, nor were carpets and some furnishing fabrics. Ballet shoes, wooden clogs (which became very popular) were not, nor were overalls and work outfits, mending yarn, shoe and boot laces, braces, hats, muslin, lint and medical garments. A quick glance through the table shows just how little you could buy during a year and, of course, the clothes had to be paid for as well as handing in the coupons.

Poorer families and those with a large number of children were the most disadvantaged but perhaps better equipped to deal with the hardship. Clothes were handed down, as they always had been, and it was often the child first up in the morning who was best dressed. In some families the shoes were shared. Kath Jarman, one of six girls, recalled how they got by on the bare minimum: 'I remember having one pair of socks and having to wash them out, iron them dry and put them on again. One of my sisters had one dress that she wore to school every day and she would wash it out every night to wear again. When girls at school mentioned it she said, "It's only my school dress. I don't wear this on a Sunday." But we accepted it, and you got used to not having anything.'[3]

Second-hand clothes sold at prices below a certain percentage of the value of the new item were available without coupons, as were clothes sold privately. Mothers were encouraged to sell or exchange clothes and shoes their children had outgrown. The WVS ran 'swap shops' primarily for children's clothes, but also for adults', particularly women's clothing. Jumble sales and markets were another source for acquiring a change of outfit. 'The "job-lot" stalls were high with shoes and coats and dresses . . . I got a lovely, thick piece of artificial crepe-de-chine for 1s 11d (9p), because it was badly soiled from dropping on a dusty floor. It will make either a blouse or a petticoat-slip.'[4]

If people living in the country fared better when it came to food, urban dwellers had more choice when buying clothes. Clothing coupons could be used anywhere; it was not necessary to be registered with a retailer as it was for food. But the government not only restricted the amount of clothing a person could buy; as supplies of cloth and other raw materials became more scarce and more of the garment industry's output was required for military production, it intervened in the manufacture of garments. Manufacturers were restricted to producing only a limited range of clothes to be sold at a reasonable price. Utility Clothing, with a distinctive CC41 label, was introduced in 1941. Later, as all manner of raw materials became in increasingly short supply, the utility range was extended to include furniture and soft furnishings, with Utility Furniture in production until 1952.

The limited range of clothing made for longer runs, but choice was restricted, and for each item the amount of material used and the styling were prescribed. There was a maximum length for men's shirts, a ban on trouser turn-ups, and a suit (single-breasted only) could have a maximum of only three pockets. Calf-length socks were replaced by ankle socks. Women's clothes could not have elasticated waistbands, and no unnecessary pleats or gathers, no fashionable belts, trimmings or embroidery. Skirts were just below the knee and fairly straight; jackets were straight and square-shouldered. Colours were limited as chemicals used for dyeing were needed for the war effort. Underwear and pyjama styles were restricted too. These were certainly not elegant or sexy, but functional – and they lasted. Short trousers were the norm for boys of all ages; they needed fewer coupons and were easier to look after and repair.

Women were not to be defeated by utility clothing; they still cared about looking stylish. Nylon and silk stockings were no longer available, so they dyed their legs with tea, and drew lines down the backs of their legs with an eyebrow pencil to imitate stocking seams. Later on, leg make-up appeared on the market. Hats, bags and gloves were what made an outfit, and since hats were off coupon, as were feathers and certain trimmings, some stylish home-made hats appeared. Wedge-soled shoes came onto the market with the increasing shortage of leather. Cork and other thick materials were used to make the soles. They were clumpy, but comfortable and hard-wearing.

As more and more women worked outside the home, many of them on the land or in factories, they started to wear utility dungarees or trousers, clothing that for most would have been unthinkable before the war. By 1944 the sales of women's trousers had increased hugely over the previous year. Trousers were here to stay as women's wear, and towards the end of the war, teenagers (although they had yet to be defined as such) first began to be seen in jeans and baggy sweaters. The turban became popular headgear; originally used to cover hair while working in factories, its practicality meant its use soon spread to other occasions.

The government realized that people had to learn how to make the best use and get the most wear out of the clothes they had. They issued leaflets on letting out and lengthening children's clothes or cutting down adult clothes to fit them, giving new life to a blouse or skirt, making new trimmings, collars or cuffs. Some dealt with more basic repairs like darning, relining pockets and patching, and decorative elbow patches became quite fashionable. The best ways to wash and care for different fabrics were also covered, as was how to ensure moths did not get into your clothes. It was just as important to keep household linen in use by cutting sheets and turning them sides-to-middle, and mending or patching sheets and blankets. If sheets were really worn out, there were always parts that could be made into handkerchiefs or bandages. Local councils set up evening classes to help women with sewing, showing them how to repair and restyle clothes.

Many other goods we take for granted – string, paper, pens and pencils, soap and washing powder – were in short supply. Keeping clothes and household linen clean became a real problem when washing powder virtually disappeared and soap was rationed to a small bar a month. Some medicines were unavailable and pharmacists resorted to knowledgeable herb gatherers in the countryside for medicinal plants like foxgloves, nettles and nightshade.

Inevitably rationing led to black-market racketeering; it didn't take long for the criminal gangs to turn their attention to ports where imported foods and clothing were unloaded, and ensure that a proportion 'disappeared' to contacts outside. When caught the criminals were sentenced to penal servitude (hard labour).

Among the population at large, pilfering from work was commonplace, as was agreeing to pay a little more for an extra ration of meat or butter, or buying something on a street corner, no questions asked about its origins. Supplies decreased severely as the war went on, and more people bought from unlicensed sources to supplement their rations. The government exhorted people to regard rationing as 'fair shares' for all, and as a system that they should defend because 'trying to beat the ration is the same as trying to cheat the nation'.

More than anything else, however, wartime shortages on the domestic front will always be best remembered for the government's anti-waste and 'Make-do and Mend' campaigns. Encouraging people's resourcefulness with salvaging and recycling has a definite resonance in the twenty-first century where so many of us are beginning to wage a war on waste through the crusade for ecologically sound living. While no one today is likely to try reinforcing their knickers for extra wear as suggested in the What Mothers Can Do . . . leaflet, perhaps there are still a few tricks to be learned about thrifty living for the modern age within the pages of *Make Do and Mend*.

JILL NORMAN

[1] Mrs Arthur Webb, *War-time Cookery*, 1939.

[2] *Nella Last's War*, 2006. The Mass Observation project was started in 1937 to create 'an anthropology of ourselves'. Volunteers were recruited to study the everyday lives of ordinary Britons, and other people kept diaries or responded to questionnaires from a central team of observers. The archives of the project are housed at the University of Sussex.

[3] Alison Maloney, *The Forties*, 2005.

[4] Nella Last, as above.

WHAT MOTHERS CAN DO TO SAVE BUYING NEW

Reinforcing children's clothes

One of the first things to remember is that reinforced clothes last twice as long. This applies particularly to children's clothes which receive such a lot of wear and tear—and they should be reinforced when they are first new.

HERE ARE ONE OR TWO SUGGESTIONS

KNICKERS

The seats of knickers and trousers should be strengthened by patching on the inside — the shape of the patch is shown on the sketch. Patches should be kept in position by herringbone stitch. When there is already a lining they should be fixed as an interlining.

SOCKS

Hand - knitted socks should have the heels and toes knitted either in double wool, or with one thread of wool and another of strong cotton thread. A similar idea is to darn stockings at the heel and toe

before being worn and the centre back seam should be firmly oversewn on the inside of the heel.

SCHOOL CLOTHES

Wait until existing clothes are really worn out (if your child is just starting school) before buying the uniform. When children approach school-leaving age—buy clothes that are suitable for post-school wear. When the uniform has been discarded for school wear simple alterations can completely change its appearance.

When considering the question of reinforcing, particular attention should be focused on schoolchildren's clothes. Schoolgirls' blouses for instance, wear particularly quickly on desks and should be reinforced with a semicircle of material at the elbow and strengthened across the back. Schoolboys' jackets can be bound at the elbows, useful material is the leather from worn-out gloves.

HOW TO LET OUT AND LENGTHEN CHILDREN'S CLOTHES

There are a wealth of ideas for letting out children's clothes, the ideas shown in the sketches are a few of the simpler ones. As a general rule, however, the outgrown article should be completely unpicked from hem to underarm each side, and then along the sleeve seam, until the whole garment can be opened out flat in one piece. Contrasting bands of material can then be let in at the sides, at the waist, and a new yoke can be made both to lengthen the frock and to let it out under the arms.

HINTS ON CUTTING NEW CLOTHES FOR CHILDREN

Leave good turnings on the following parts when cutting out new clothes for children : side seams, top edges of skirts and trousers and lower edges of bodices, underarm seams of sleeves in one-piece sleeves (both seams in two-piece sleeves), across the shoulders, centre back seams on coats and jackets, also at hems, cuffs and trousers hems. Leave the extra material inside the seams of the garment when making it up, so that at some future date it can be used for letting out.

In the case of a one-piece garment like a sleeping suit, allow for a deep tuck at the waistline, and in the case of a dress with a yoke, leave material under the yoke.

Always make and buy children's clothes on the big side.

CUTTING DOWN GROWN-UPS CLOTHES FOR CHILDREN

Never cut up clothes until they are really beyond repair.

If you are not an expert, always use a pattern when you cut down grown-ups' clothes for children. Hold the material up to the light to find the weak spots and mark with a ring of coloured tackings any worn parts that would not last long. Having unpicked the garment, wash and press all the pieces, then arrange the pattern on them, avoiding any of the marked places. Make up as you would a new garment. Don't be afraid of using different materials or colours (so long as they wash the same way). Sleeves of non-matching material look perfectly well and the bodice of a dress can be different from a skirt.

Some of the following are suggested as ideas:—

Men's jackets into small girl's or boy's overcoats and jackets.

Men's pyjamas into small children's underclothes, sleeping suits, nightdresses, overalls, blouses and shirts or summer frocks.

Men's old shirts into dresses, blouses, underclothes and nightgowns.

★ Most women's clothes can be cut down for children into dresses, coats, toddlers' suits and underclothes.

SHOES AND SLIPPERS

Slippers of all sizes can be made from old felt hats, pieces of thick cloth, etc. The best way is to take a pattern of the foot on a sheet of newspaper, drawing a line round it, and allowing an $\frac{1}{8}$ in. turning—the top pieces should also be cut to pattern.

LOOKING AFTER SHOES

Remind children to wear slippers in the house, as it does save kicking out at the toes and sitting with leather shoes in front of a fire. If your child has Wellingtons see that they are only worn when it is raining — rubber is scarce, and they are an asset which may become difficult to possess. Always see that shoe-laces are untied before the children kick off their shoes.

SHOE AND CLOTHING EXCHANGES

In many cupboards throughout the country, children's shoes are lying idle not because they are outworn but simply because they are outgrown. Local schools, welfare clinics or women's organisations arrange for exchanges of outgrown shoes.

Printed for H.M. Stationery Office by Cockayne & Co., Ltd., London, S.E.1—T51—3910   B.O.T.—3.L

HOW TO DARN HOLES AND TEARS

by Mrs. SEW-and-SEW

● Do not wait for holes to develop. It is better to darn as soon as garments begin to wear thin. Imitate, as well as possible, the texture of the fabric being darned. When darning a big hole, tack a piece of net at the back and darn across it, and this will give an extra support for the stitches. A tear should be tacked round on to a piece of paper, to hold the edges in position.

DARNING A HOLE

First clear the loops of fluff and broken ends of threads from knitted garments or clip away ragged edges from machine knit fabrics. Always use a darning ball under large holes.

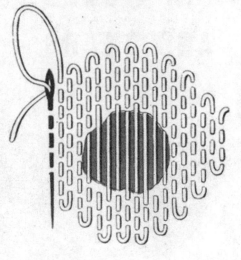

1. Make the darn the shape of the hole.
2. Darn up and down the hole first ; work on the wrong side.
3. Choose mending as fine as the material of the garment.
4. Begin a good distance away from the hole in order to reinforce the thin parts round the hole.
5. Space the rows of darning the width of a strand of mending apart.
6. Pick up the backs of the loops only unless the material is very fine.
7. Leave loops at the ends of each row and darn so that stitches alternate with spaces between stitches in the previous rows.
8. Pick up the edge of the hole in one row then go over the edge of the hole in the next row. If you have cleared the edges of the hole you will find this will be easy and will make a neater mend on the right side of the garment.
9. Continue the darn over the thin place beyond the hole.

Darning over the first rows of darning

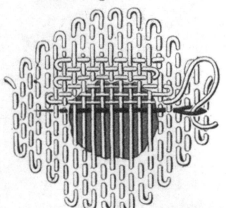

1. Darn over the hole only and about two stitches of darning beyond.
2. Leave loops at the ends of each row, and only pick up on the needle the darning stitches.
3. Pick up the alternate strands of mending in first row.
4. In alternate rows, pick up the strands of mending you passed over in the previous row.

DARNING A TEAR

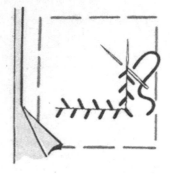

Before darning a tear, tack down on to a piece of paper and fish-bone stitch the edges of tear together.

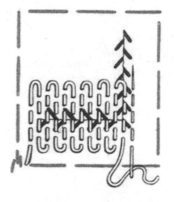

Darn well beyond tear right across base, forming a rectangle.

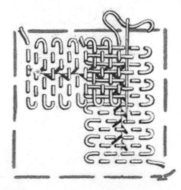

Turn the work round and darn in the same way across the other part of tear. At the corner a solid square is formed. Remove tacking thread and paper.

DARNING ON KNITTED FABRICS

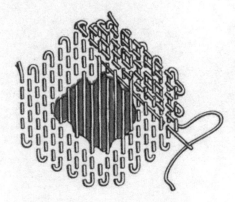

The first stage in darning on knitted fabrics is the same as an ordinary darn, but the direction of the second set of stitches is diagonal.

REINFORCING HEAVY WOOLLIES

For reinforcing heavy woollies such as knitted jumpers, etc., work on the wrong side and weave in and out following the loops of the knitting.

F3902 Wt. 44677 120,120 1/45 Gp. 961 Fosh & Cross, Ltd. Ch.L.—5

Here are your Battle Orders

Every citizen—particularly every housewife—is now in the front line in the vital Battle for Fuel. Everything possible must be done to save fuel. Here, in handy form, you will find a number of hints and suggestions on how best to make day to day savings in your home. Follow these closely and see that the other people in the house do so too. Small economies in many directions soon add up to a really worth-while saving.

1 Fuel Unit Equals

½ Cwt. of Coal or Coke or
500 Cubic Feet of Gas
or 50 Units of Electricity
or 1 Gallon of Paraffin

★ Remember, THE FUEL YEAR dates from July 1st 1942 until June 30th 1943. By referring to the chart on the back page you can work out the number of Fuel Units you are allowed. Lose no time in dividing these up among the various types of fuel you use. Some of your allowance is used up already and there is cold weather ahead—so go carefully now.

Practical Hints for :

≡ HEATING ≡

FIRE BRICKS FOR ECONOMY

Put fire bricks at the sides and back of all coal fires. This effects a great saving of fuel without seriously reducing the room temperature. Keep the fire small. Don't put on another lump after 8 p.m. Go easy with the poker.

DAMPER DRILL

Study your boiler carefully and learn how you can use it economically. Don't keep dampers and doors wide open, adjust the draught carefully. In some cases as much as 4 lbs. of coke can be saved this way each day.

ALWAYS SIFT YOUR CINDERS

They are partly-burnt coal or coke and their heat value is 7 lbs. of cinders to 5 lbs. of coal. If you have no sifter, the grate bottom may answer your purpose, otherwise pick the cinders carefully out of the debris. Everything will burn again except the ash dust.

CLEANLINESS MAKES FOR ECONOMY

Do not use a dirty wick. Clean the wick daily with a soft cloth, taking care that the charred fragments do not collect on the burner.

USE GAS AND ELECTRIC FIRES SPARINGLY

Replace any broken radiants in gas fires. These are wasteful of gas. Never use two elements in your electric fire when one will do. Keep doors of rooms closed and exclude draughts to maintain the room temperature.

'LAG' YOUR HOT WATER SYSTEM

Examine your hot water system and wherever possible cover up hot water tanks and the hot water pipes nearby with old bits of felt, thicknesses of newspaper or corrugated paper. Use string or wire to lash these or similar materials round your tanks and pipes. The object of this is to save fuel by preventing the heat from radiating into the air. You will use much less fuel and your water will keep hot much longer.

BATHTUB ECONOMY

Limit yourself to one hot bath a week. Use a bowl and a sponge on other days . . . Never have the water in the bath more than 5 ins. deep. Go easy with the geyser.

EIGHT RULES FOR USERS OF COMBINATION GRATES

• Give the words Combination Grate a new meaning by combining with your neighbour to use one fire. Do this until the cold weather comes. Get together and combine against Hitler by making one grate serve

Remember— that ¾ of your
Cooking t

two families. What hardship is this compared to Russian conditions?

- Put a fire brick in the grate on the side opposite to the oven flue.
- When using the oven or boiler, bank the fire up with slack to prevent cold air entering.
- When used only as an open fire the boiler and oven dampers should be fully closed.
- When possible the fire should be damped down with slack plus garden refuse.
- It is of great importance to keep the oven flues clean.
- Cinders down to the size of a pea ($\frac{1}{8}$ in.) should be sifted out and used again.
- Air leaks into flues should be sealed with fire cement.

TURN OFF THE HEAT

If you use a gas-heated boiler or electrical immersion heater, turn it off when the water is hot, and make do with one cylinder of hot water. Do not leave the heater running continuously.

WATCH THE WATER TAPS

Do not let taps drip. Coal is used in pumping cold water. Have all worn washers replaced. Don't wash or clean your teeth under a running tap. Don't have more water in the basin than needed.

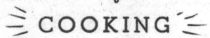

COOKING

GOLDEN RULES FOR GAS COOKERS

Never light your oven to cook a single dish. With a little planning you can easily prepare an entire meal while the oven is hot, as well as a pudding or tart that can be eaten cold next day.

Turn out the burners directly the food is done — it will keep hot in the oven for some time. Always clean your cooker regularly — burners clogged with grease are slow and extravagant. More than half the gas which is used in homes on the gas cooker, is used on the large ring. By using the small ring instead, there is a saving of over one fuel unit in ten, although the job takes longer.

Keep lids on saucepans to contain the heat. Cut down hot meals to a minimum.

WRINKLES FOR WASHING-UP

Use a small bowl . . . . Heat the water in the oven while it is cooling. . . . Do the whole day's dishes at one time.

Scrape all the plates and dishes before you start.

Never wash-up or clean vegetables under a running tap.

HOW TO MEASURE YOUR COAL AND COKE.

A two-gallon bucket holds about 12 lbs. of coal or 8 lbs. of coke.

NUMBER OF ROOMS	NORTHERN	MIDLANDS	SOUTHERN
	HOUSE ALLOWANCE IN FUEL UNITS		
1	80	60	50
2	90	70	60
3	110	90	70
4	120	100	80
5	140	110	90
6	150	120	100
7 OR MORE	170	140	110

IN ADDITION, YOUR PERSONAL FUEL ALLOWANCE is 15 fuel units per year, which equals 7½ cwts. of coal or a corresponding amount of other fuels. This applies to adults and children alike.

NORTHERN AREA COMPRISES: Lancashire (including the County Borough of Manchester), Cheshire (only Stalybridge and Hyde division), Derbyshire (only the High Peak division), Yorkshire and all Counties to the north of these. The whole of Scotland forms part of the Northern Zone.

MIDLAND AREA COMPRISES: Cardiganshire, Breconshire, Herefordshire, Worcestershire, Warwickshire, Northamptonshire, Bedfordshire, Cambridge and Suffolk, and all Counties to the north of these up to and including Cheshire (other than the Stalybridge and Hyde division), Derbyshire (other than the High Peak division), Nottinghamshire and Lincolnshire.

SOUTHERN AREA COMPRISES: Pembrokeshire, Monmouthshire, Carmarthen, Glamorgan, Gloucestershire, Oxfordshire, Buckinghamshire, Hertfordshire and Essex, Middlesex, Berkshire, Kent, Surrey, Sussex, Hampshire, Wiltshire, Dorset, Somerset, Devon, Cornwall, and the whole of the County of London.

HOW TO READ YOUR GAS METER

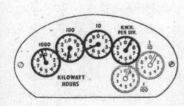

On your meter you will see one test dial and below it a row of three or four recording dials. *Ignore the top dial.* Take each dial from left to right and write down the *smaller* of the two figures between which the pointers stand. If the pointer is between 0 and 1, write down 0; but if between 9 and 0, write down 9. Do this with each dial. Add 00 after the figures and you have the present meter reading in cubic feet. Deduct the figure of the previous reading and you have the gas consumption for the period between the two readings.

(The dials shown here read: 751900 *cubic feet*)

HOW TO READ YOUR ELECTRICITY METER

Disregard the two right-hand dials. Of the other four, the first at the left represents thousands, the next hundreds, the next tens; and the fourth, single units or kilowatt hours. The hands in adjacent dials revolve in opposite directions. Begin reading at the single unit dial. When the hand is between two figures, write down the lower figure; when the hand is between 0 and 9, write down 9. Go through the same process with the other dials, writing the figures down from *right to left*. Keep a record of your reading and when next you read the meter, subtract the old figure from the new. The result is your unit consumption for that period.

(The dials shown here read: 9469 *units*)

HELP WIN THE BATTLE FOR FUEL

PRINTED FOR H.M. STATIONERY OFFICE BY FOSH & CROSS, LTD. 51/2809   ISSUED BY THE MINISTRY OF FUEL & POWER.

HOW TO LOOK AFTER RAYON

Nowadays our clothes must last longer —we must "make do and mend." Washing and ironing play an important part in the life of all fabrics. Rayon for instance can be washed time and time again and very simply too. This is because it only soils on the surface, with the result that Rayon fabrics or garments or stockings can be quickly and easily restored to their original freshness and loveliness.

WASHING . . .   . . . IRONING

Use warm water and see that the soap is thoroughly dissolved and whisked into a good lather. Dip and squeeze thoroughly in the suds without rubbing or wringing — the dirt will come away easily. Rinse two or three times (without wringing or twisting) in order to remove all traces of soap. After the final rinsing, squeeze the material and then roll in a towel to dry off excess moisture. If hung up to dry, see that the garment is opened out in order to distribute the wet weight and to avoid uneven drying. Coloured rayons should be dried at once and never left bunched up. When drying out of doors choose a shady place, not direct sunlight. Wash any specially dirty marks before putting the whole garment into water. *

Before ironing pull the garment gently into shape. If it has become too dry, rinse it through again. Never sprinkle rayons with water, as patches will occur.

*

Use a warm (not hot) iron. The correct temperature can be tested by standing the iron on a newspaper for 15 to 20 seconds. If the paper scorches, the iron is too hot. Rayon should be ironed on the wrong side and only one thickness at a time, taking care not to press buttons or fastenings into the fabric. Seams should be pressed thoroughly dry or they may contract and spoil the shape of the garment.

Wash rayon stockings daily. Dry thoroughly but don't iron. Rinse a new pair before wearing for the first time.

Overleaf you will see at a glance how the different surfaces should be treated.

DULL & SUEDE FINISH RAYONS

Iron nearly dry.

RAYON MAROCAINS

Iron fairly damp, stretching the material both ways as you iron—to counteract a temporary shrinkage in washing.

RAYON GEORGETTE

All georgettes have a tendency to shrink when wet so iron on a well-padded board stretching the fabric gently both ways as you iron.

RAYON SATIN

Iron on the wrong side when fairly damp, then finish very lightly on the right side.

KNITTED RAYONS

If ironing do so when almost dry and across the garment first in order to prevent dropping.

FLANNEL-TYPE SPUN RAYON

Press with a damp cloth when nearly dry.

LINEN-TYPE SPUN RAYON

Iron fairly damp.

WHEN MENDING...

Never patch old material with new if you can help it. If you do use new, however, wash the patch piece first. Cut out all the good parts of a worn garment and keep them for patching.

If a garment splits at the seam, don't just try sewing up the seam again, that will only make the garment tighter and if it has split it is probably a little too tight anyway. Put a small patch down the seam instead—a scrap of ribbon is a very good thing to use for this.

Mend any hole or thin place as soon as it appears. Very large holes in the foot of a stocking should be patched rather than darned. Use a piece of an old stocking, lay it on the wrong side of the stocking that is to be mended and "herring bone" the edges down on both sides.

AND MAKING DO...

The tops of nightdresses usually wear out first. Cut the skirts down into slips or knickers.

*　　*　　*

Camiknickers that have gone at the top can be cut down into knickers. And those that have gone in the legs can be cut off just below the waist to make what used to be called a "chemise." You will find that a "Chemise and Knicker" set made from two old camiknickers will give you a great deal more wear.

*　　*　　*

Convert a slip into camiknickers in this way. Cut the slip to the right length, using the odd pieces to make a rectangle about 8″ x 4″. Seam round the rectangle. Sew one end across the centre back of your slip—and fasten two lengths of ribbon to the other corners and sew into the front of the skirt. You will need no buttons or press studs.

A useful skirt can be made from a dress, the bodice of which is past repair. Cut it away at the waist—make a side placket and mount it on a petersham band. The best parts of the bodice can be cut into a belt to finish the waistline or to make patch pockets on the hips. Pocket patches would hide any defects in the front.

*　　*　　*

An old skirt will make one pair of knickers and a little play suit for a seven–year–old.

*　　*　　*

Pyjama legs will make children's vests. Washing-silk dresses make up into gay pyjamas for children.

*　　*　　*

Quite small scraps of material left over from worn slips and knickers can be used for making brassieres. Use an old, well-fitting brassiere for a pattern.

HOW TO PATCH AN OVERALL

by Mrs. SEW-and-SEW

Patching material for an overall may be cut from the lining of yoke, belt, pocket, cuffs or collar. The sleeves and hem could be shortened. If you are patching patterned material, always match design perfectly and hem very neatly and the result will be almost invisible. Contrasting cloth can be used to replace a part that is cut away, and pieces of the overall can be put by for future patching

Showing areas useful for patching

Cut patch to extend well over arm-hole and side seam. Match pattern carefully

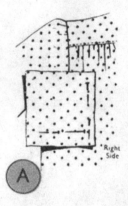

Right Side

A

Right Side

B

Unpick arm-hole and side seam for inserting patch

Tack down on right side and hem the straight edges

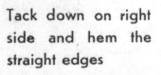

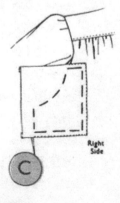

Right Side

C

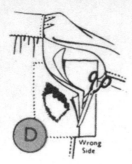

Cut patch to the shape of overall using the worn part as a pattern, the un-picked seams show turnings required

Then cut away worn part leaving $\frac{1}{4}$ inch turnings and blanket-stitch edges

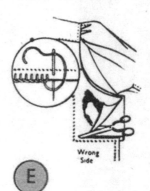

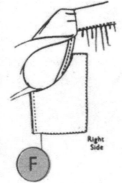

Re-make under-arm French seam by put-ting the two edges together on the right side first

Complete French seam by running on wrong side

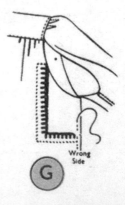

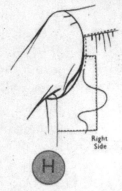

First stage of French seam for arm-hole from right side

Right Side

H

French seam completed on wrong side

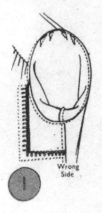

Wrong Side

I

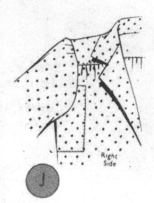

Finished patch should be almost invisible if well pressed

Right Side

J

Contrasting pieces forming trimming and substituting pieces used for patches

YOUR HOUSEHOLD LINEN HAS GOT TO LAST !

Here are some useful suggestions . . .

STORAGE

If you have some linen which is not in use, store it away—but not in a hot cupboard and not if it is starched. For long storage wrap in paper parcels—and place in a cool but dry chest, cupboard or drawer. Wash, mend and air before putting it away. Refold at intervals to prevent wear at the creases. Only store clean linen.

MENDING

There is a lot of wear left in linens which look worn and every ounce of wear must be got out of them. Hold sheets, pillowcases and towels up to a strong light and look through them—this will often show up tiny holes and slits—such as cuts made by razor blades, which are almost invisible before the towel is washed, but become large ragged tears afterwards. Be sure that if pillowcase buttons are hanging loose they are taken off before sending it to the wash.

When patching use old material—a new patch on a worn towel for instance is liable to tear it away. Always mend linen before it is washed—if you haven't time to do so properly, draw it together roughly for the time being with an oversewing stitch. Thin spots should be reinforced by darning, either by hand or machine before they actually wear into holes. A two-sided tear should be darned in both directions, so that the place of the tear is doubly darned.

SHEETS AND PILLOW CASES

● When sheets get very thin, turn them sides to middle by cutting them lengthways down the centre, and either over-sewing the outside selvedges together or joining them with a run and fell seam. Trim away the torn parts of what are now the sides of the sheet. Turn in the edges and hem them.

● If a sheet already turned sides-to-middle has become too thin to use, wait until you have another one in the same condition, then join the two together. Place them smoothly one on top of the other, then sew them together down the centre with a row of running stitches. To prevent uncomfortable wrinkles, the sheets must be "locked" together. Do this by smoothing the two from the stitching outwards, then running another line of stitching down the sheet parallel with the first line. Do the same on the other side, spacing the lines of stitching about 12 in. apart until the sides are reached. Oversew the outside edges of the sheets together and darn any small holes or thin patches through both thicknesses of material.

● One fair sized sheet can be made to do the work of two by cutting a line about 18 in. long down the centre of the top—these edges should be hemmed. The sheet can then be used double on a small bed, the slit allowing the top to be turned back over the blankets without difficulty.

● Hemstitched borders on pillows or pillowcases can be mended by tacking the two edges on to strong paper, leaving a narrow channel between, and joining the two with faggot stitch. The simplest form of faggot stitch is just a bar with the thread twisted round it.

● When pillowcases get too thin to be used without risk of tearing, join the front and back together with rows of running stitching as in the illustration—then add a false back of any washing material, and slip in the pillow in the ordinary way.

● Bolster cases are not essential nowadays—the bolster can be covered with the lower sheet. If you are short of pillowcases unpick the seam that runs the length of the bolster, fold the material over, so that the two ends come together, and rejoin the two sides to form a pillow-case.

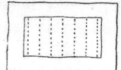

TOWELS

Thin places and small holes can be reinforced by machine darning or by hand darning with soft mending cotton.

Large holes should be patched with the sound parts of other old towelling — never use new material. Patches on towels should be tacked in position without the edge of the patch being turned in. These edges should then be stitched on to the towel with herringbone or cross-stitch.

If you haven't a towel rail, fix a

loop to two diagonal corners of the towel so that it can be hung up without being damaged—change the loop it is hanging on from time to time—this will equalize wear—as towels are bound to be used while they are hanging on a hook.

Sew two thin tea towels together, arranging that the holes in the one are covered with the sound part of the other cloth.

When dusters wear thin, sew two together round the edge and several times across the centre.

WASHING HINTS

1 Mend all holes and tears before washing—whether they are done at home or at the laundry. If you haven't time to do a proper darn catch tears together. Laundries are working under difficulties these days and a stitch in time will be appreciated.

2 Most stains can be removed if dealt with *at once* by using plain tepid water.

3 Never let clothes or household linens get really dirty; several gentle washes are less harmful than one hard one and use soft water—rain water is best.

4 Separate whites from coloureds and soak dirty whites overnight in soapy water. Dissolve the soap in a separate jar of very hot water, to make a lather and then add it to the cold water in which the linen is to be soaked.

5 It is better not to boil linen and cottons and never boil coloureds. If whites have to be boiled and the water is hard, add soda in proportion of $\frac{1}{2}$ oz. to 5 or 6 gallons of hot water. Leave for a few minutes and then avoid bleaching which is an expert's job—dry in the sun instead.

6 Wash in hot soapy water using only sufficient soap to make a lather. Note any particularly dirty parts before putting the things into the water. These can then be rubbed with hard soap.

7 Rinse thoroughly until the water is clear, and dry out of doors when possible—the whites in the sun and the coloureds in the shade. Roll up for ironing when still slightly damp.

If the things are bone dry sprinkle them with water and roll them up an hour before ironing.

 I R O N I N G

Sheets and pillowcases need very little ironing if they have been mangled after being folded into shape. Towels need not be ironed at all; rough drying saves fuel and wear. Always use a hot iron and plenty of pressure for ironing cotton and linen and never iron the folds.

Mend and Make-do to save buying new

Printed for H.M. Stationery Office by Cockayne & Co., Ltd., London, S.E.1—T.51–3895

Simple
HOUSEHOLD
REPAIRS and
how to handle
them

Why not be your own " handy man ", now that skilled labour has so many wartime calls upon it? Odd jobs like these are easier than you would think—don't send out for someone to attend to them till you have had a good try yourself.

BLACKOUT CURTAINS AGEING?

Care and repair will do wonders in making your blackout last out. *Never wash blackout material*—washing makes it more apt to let the light through. Instead, go over your curtains regularly with a vacuum cleaner if you have one ; if not, take them down at least twice a year, shake gently and brush well. Then iron them thoroughly—this makes them more light proof and also kills any moth eggs or grubs which may be in them.

Keep curtain rings sewn on and hems sewn up. Mend a rent before it has a chance to grow. And where a curtain is fixed with tacks, reinforce the hem with odd scraps of material to help it stand the strain.

FURNITURE HANDLES OFF ?

Where handles have become loose or detached, remove all the fixing screws and plug the screw holes with used match-sticks or plugs cut from firewood, etc. Glue the plugs and drive them firmly into the screw-holes. Level off the projecting ends of the plugs and refix the handles with screws in the original positions.

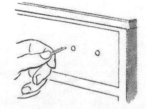

Adhesive for wood plugs is readily obtainable in small tubes from most oilshops or ironmongers.

A CARPET TO PATCH?

Cut away the worn part allowing 1 inch all round for turnings. Remove the pile from this 1 inch allowance and fray the threads. Group these threads and fasten with carpet thread on the wrong side. Cut a piece of carpet 1 inch larger than the hole, matching the design, if any. Remove the pile and fray the edge of 1 inch all round. Turn these threads on to the wrong side and secure as before. Fix the patch into the hole and stitch at the four corners. Blanket stitch the patch to the carpet, stitching on alternative sides of the join. When finished, press the patch on the wrong side with a warm iron.

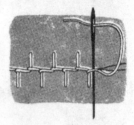

Worn carpets may also be repaired by knotting wool through the threadbare backing and then cutting to the length of the existing pile.

CHAIR SEAT TO RE-WEB?

Carefully remove the covering, stuffing and webs from the seat frame, and lever out the nails with the end of an old screwdriver. Tack on new webbing in the same positions as the old, but do not drive the tacks into the old holes. Each web should be doubled under ½ inch at one end and fixed with three tacks. To stretch the web, grip the free end with a pair of pincers held against the edge of the seat frame and lever downwards. Drive in three tacks to hold it taut, cut off the web 1 inch beyond the outer tacks, double the cut end and secure to the frame with two tacks. The webs should be interlaced. ⅝-inch tacks are suitable. Replace the stuffing carefully and refix to cover.

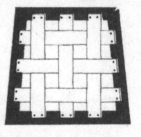

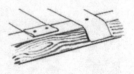

Table leg to Mend ?

Where a table or chair leg has broken *diagonally* below the level of the rails connecting the legs, a satisfactory repair can be carried out by warming the broken ends of the leg, well glueing the fracture and pressing the two pieces firmly together. Wipe off the surplus glue with a clean rag soaked in warm water and tightly bind the joint with string. When the glue in the joint has set (allow 24 hours undisturbed) remove the string, soak off if necessary, and clean the joint with a wet rag as before.

In cases *where the leg has snapped off across the grain of the wood*, a temporary repair may be effected as follows :—

Turn the table or chair upside down in a

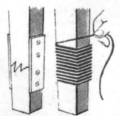

level position, warm and glue the fracture as previously described, then press the broken leg very firmly downwards until the fractured ends engage closely. Leave the joint undisturbed for 24 hours, then clean off the surplus glue. Prepare two tablets of hardwood or plywood about 4 inches to 5 inches long, ¼ inch thick, and of a width equal to that of the leg. Bore a suitable number of holes in each tablet and screw them on opposite faces of the leg. An equal number of screws should be inserted above and below the fracture and no screws should be inserted within 1 inch of the joint. The edges of the tablets can be smoothed off and the tablets stained if desired.

SINK STOPPED UP?

As a first effort allow 3 inches or 4 inches of water to remain in the sink and using the palm of the hand or a swabbing cloth over the outlet, quickly plunge it up and down. This will usually move the obstruction.

If this does not work, place a pail under the screw cap at the bottom of the U bend or trap and undo this cap with the aid of a strong bar—a screwdriver shaft, say. A rush of water will come directly the cap is off and it will bring accumulation of hair, etc., with it. But if the pipe is still stopped up, poke it clear with a stick inserted from the open end of the trap on both sides. Be sure to screw cap on again securely. Remember that frequently unscrewing of the cap spoils the thread of the screw—try and keep the sink clean in the first place by frequently swilling with soda and hot water.

WALLPAPER *torn or soiled?*

When a papered wall is damaged the paper can be patched so that it is hardly noticeable. Remove the torn or stained bit where loose. Cut out a piece of wallpaper rather larger than that you have removed and tear the edge so that it is rough and irregular—this makes the patch inconspicuous. Paste on carefully.

Broomhead Loose! Take out the handle and saw off an inch or so of the worn part where it has been split by the nail. Then refix the head and nail firmly in position. Never put brooms and brushes away standing on their heads.

LITTLE LEAKS?

Small repairs to enamel jugs and basins that are not used for hot liquid, can be done with sealing wax. Clean and dry the leaky part and melt a stick of matching sealing wax over the worn surface, pressing it down well.

Saucepan needing Repair?

To repair a leaky pot or kettle, get a soldering iron, a stick of solder and some flux—these can be bought at an ironmongers. Empty the kettle, dry the outside thoroughly, and rub well around the hole with emery paper, to make sure the surface is absolutely clean. Put the soldering iron into a clear fire or in the flame of a gas ring, to heat. Smear the place to be mended with flux and when the iron is really hot (don't however let it get red-hot), dip it into the flux, pick up the stick of solder and hold this over the hole, let the tip of the hot iron touch the end of the solder so that it melts and runs down into the hole. Rub the top of the iron over the solder on the kettle until the hole is filled in. If it is a large hole, hold a piece of sheet metal, which need not be cleaned, underneath to prevent the solder falling through. Remember that *except for aluminium or cast iron*, most kitchen utensils can be mended by this method. For a tin kettle, an ordinary pot-mender may be simpler and safer than soldering.

LEAKY ALUMINIUM?

You cannot solder aluminium or cast iron, but small holes can usually be repaired with an aluminium rivet, unless the hole is on an actual seam. Insert the rivet into the hole, then tap gently with a hammer on and around the rivet so that it expands to fit the hole and so that a head is formed.

Fuse Blown?

First turn off the main switch. Then examine the fuse box for the carrier that has failed—it may be blackened and the wire on it will be severed. Free the broken ends of wire by loosening the small screws holding them to the carrier. Put a new piece of wire, of the same gauge as the old, into position by twisting it round the top screw clockwise. Tighten both screws, replace carrier, close the fuse box and switch on the current.

Note : Fuse wire in most common use is for 5, 10 or 15 amp. loading, and the carrier or the fuse box will generally indicate which wire must be fitted. Cards of fuse wire for the three loadings named are easily obtainable from an electrician. Make certain that you use the correct wire.

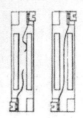

POTMENDER NEEDED?

Small holes in buckets, kettles, etc., can be stopped quite easily with " pot-menders " from the ironmongers. The discs should be fixed on each side of the hole, with the cork on the inside of the utensil between the discs. The screw and nut will hold them together.

Flex Frayed?

The connecting leads for reading lamps, electric wires, etc., often wear so that the wire itself is exposed. This is dangerous. Bind with cotton or thread—and secure the end of the binding to prevent its coming undone.

IT'S AS EASY AS A.B.C.

— IF YOU KNOW HOW

Any job goes better if you understand just how to set about it. Many women are experts with hammer and nails these days—but many others will find the following hints very useful.

IN DRIVING A NAIL, decide first whether it is to go in straight or at an angle ; then when striking the nail always keep the hammer in the line you have decided on.

WHEN PUTTING IN A SCREW, make a hole first with a small gimlet and bore to about half the length of the screw. This will give you a good start.

WHEN MAKING A JOIN you will get extra strength by driving in two nails in a V shape where the corners come together. See diagram.

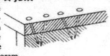

TO FIX A HOOK OR SCREW to a brick or concrete wall, first tap a hole with a cold chisel. Cut a wooden plug slightly larger than the hole and drive it in securely. Trim off flush with the wall, then bore a hole with a gimlet in the plug and proceed to fix the hook or screw.

TO EXTRACT A NAIL with a claw hammer, put a piece of wood under the hammer head to give leverage. See diagram. This makes the job easier and prevents marking the wood from which the nail is drawn.

A LOOSE HAMMER HEAD can be tightened temporarily by soaking it in water so that the wood swells. A more lasting repair can be made by driving a short nail or wedge into the top of the handle where it shows through the hammer head.

Make the most of your SEWING TIME

—by taking your work along to your nearest Make-do and Mend Class. All the difficult bits—cutting out, renovating, etc.—are made easier for you there. Your local Evening Institute, Technical College, or Woman's Organisation is probably running a class now. Or ask at the Citizens' Advice Bureaux—they'll tell you where and when these classes meet.

(F.2955) Wt.9033 100,000 4/44 Gp.961 Fosh & Cross Ltd.   B.O.T. IIL.

HOW TO PATCH ELBOWS AND TROUSERS

by Mrs. SEW-and-SEW

● It is easy to mend the elbow of a two seam sleeve, as the worn part can be cut away and all that will be seen is the seam at the top of the new section. Do not use new material, as it will be of a much heavier texture than the worn garment. Cut the best parts of old garments and keep them by you for future patching. New coats and knickers can be strengthened before wearing by patching neatly on the wrong side.

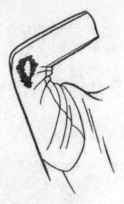

● A two seam sleeve with hole and thin area at elbow.

Ⓐ   Right Side

● Cloth for patch should extend well beyond hole, seams and cuff.

Ⓑ   Wrong Side

● Unpick lining and seams to the top level of patch.

● Sew patch on by placing right sides together to give a flat pressed seam on the wrong side.

Ⓒ   Right Side

● Trim new section to the shape of the worn sleeve.

(D) Wrong Side

● Notch seams, press open, catch-stitch turning at wrist.

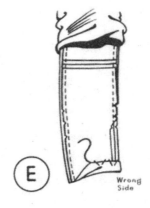

(E) Wrong Side

● Replace lining, hem lower edge to wrist.

(F)

● There is another method of patching elbows. This is quite easy to do and needs only a small piece of material. The patch can be woven into the material by darning the frayed edges of the patch into the garment. Details of this are given in the Board of Trade Make Do and Mend booklet on page 11.

When linings begin to wear they can be patched as shown here.

Wrong Side

Before beginning patch unpick seams. Patch both sides to match for the sake of appearances.

Use a round patch and do not cut away the worn part, as this helps to re-inforce the new patch.

F3883. Wt. 43681 120,120 12/44 Gp. 961 Fosh & Cross Ltd. CHL-3

AFTER
THE
RAID

ISSUED BY THE MINISTRY OF HOME SECURITY
LONDON REGION EDITION   DECEMBER, 1940

AFTER THE RAID

WHEN YOU HAVE been in the front line and taken it extra hard the country wants to look after you. For you have suffered in the national interest as well as in your own in the fight against Hitler. If your home is damaged there is a great deal of help ready for you.

You will want to know where this help can be found and whom to ask about it. Here are some hints about how you stand. Remember, in reading them, that conditions are different in different areas and the services may not always be quite the same.

HAVE YOUR PLANS READY

YOU SHOULD TRY to make plans *now* to go and stay with friends or relations living near, but not too near, *in case your house is destroyed.* They should also arrange *now* to come to you if their house is knocked out.

If you have to go and stay with them until you can make more permanent arrangements the Government will pay them a lodging allowance of 5s. per week for each adult and 3s. for each child. Your host should enquire at the Town Hall or Council offices about this.

Your local authority will be setting up an Administrative Centre where your questions can be answered. Look out for posters telling you where this centre is or ask the police or wardens for the address. In the meantime, in case of emergency, find out from the police or wardens where the offices are at which the local authority and the Assistance Board are doing their work for people who have been bombed.

FOOD AND SHELTER

IF YOU HAVE NOT been able to make arrangements with friends or relatives and have *nowhere to sleep and eat* after your house has been destroyed, the best thing to do is to go to an emergency *Rest Centre*. The wardens and policemen will tell you where this is. You will get food and shelter there until you can go home or make other arrangements. You will also find at the Rest Centre an officer whose job it is to help you with your problems. He will tell you how to get *clothes* if you've lost your own, *money*—if you are in need—a new ration book, a new identity card, a new gas mask, etc. Nurses will be there, too, to help with children and anybody who is suffering from shock.

NEW HOMES FOR THE HOMELESS

A HOME WILL BE FOUND for you, if you cannot make your own arrangements. If you are still earning your normal wages you may have to pay rent.

If you have had to leave your home and can make arrangements to go and stay with friends or relatives you will be given a free travel voucher, if you cannot get to them without help. Enquire about this at the Rest Centre or Administrative Centre (or if there is no Administrative Centre, at the Town Hall or Council offices).

TRACING FRIENDS AND RELATIVES

TO KEEP IN TOUCH with your friends and relatives you should, if you find your own accommodation, send your new address to the Secretary, London Council of Social Service,

7, Bayley Street, Bedford Square, London, W.C.1.
Of course, also tell your friends and relatives
where you are.

Anyone who is homeless and has been provided
with accommodation can be found through the
Town Halls, the Council offices and the Citizens'
Advice Bureaux, since records are kept. If you
have got sons or daughters in the Army, Navy,
R.A.F., or the Auxiliary Services, they can find
you, too, through their Commanding Officer,
wherever you may be—whether you have gone to
the country, are in hospital or are with friends.
In the London area through the local authorities
and through the Citizens' Advice Bureaux the
Director of Welfare in the London and Eastern
Commands is helping men and women serving in
the Forces to maintain contact with their relations
who may have had to move.

FURNITURE AND OTHER BELONGINGS

(1) *If your income is below a certain amount* you
can apply to the Assistance Board for :—

> (*a*) a grant to replace *essential* furniture* and
> *essential* household articles ;
>
> (*b*) a grant to replace your clothes† or those of
> your family ;
>
> (*c*) a grant to replace *tools*† essential to your
> work.

You also have a claim for your other belongings,
but these do not come under the Assistance
Board's scheme, and you should make your claim
on Form V.O W.1.‡

* The household income must be normally £400 a year or
less (*i.e.*, nearly £8 0s. 0d. per week or less).
† Your income in this case must be normally £250 a year or
less (*i.e.*, nearly £5 0s. 0d. per week or less) or £400 a year or
less if you have dependants.
‡ You can get this form at your Town Hall or the offices
of your Council.

3

(2) *If your income is above certain limits*, you do not come under the Assistance Board's scheme and should make out a claim for all your belongings on Form V.O.W.1.*

The time at which payment can be made for belongings not covered by the Assistance Board's scheme will be settled shortly, when Parliament has passed the War Damage Bill.

(3) If bombing has left you without any *ready cash*, because you have lost your job or cannot get to work to be paid or because you have been hurt, you can apply to the Assistance Board.

COMPENSATION FOR DAMAGE TO HOUSES

IF YOU *own your house* or hold it on a long lease and it is damaged or destroyed, whatever your income, you should, as soon as possible, make a claim on Form V.O.W.1.* The amount of your compensation and the time of paying it will depend on the passing of the War Damage Bill now before Parliament.

REPAIRS

IF YOUR HOUSE can be made fit to live in with a few simple repairs the local authority (apply to the Borough or Council Engineer) will put it right if the landlord is not able to do it. But how quickly the local authority can do this depends on local conditions.

FOOD

If your gas is cut off, or your kitchen range is out of action, then you may be able to get hot meals at the Londoners' Meals Service restaurants in the

---

* You can get this form at your Town Hall or the offices of your Council.

4

London County Council area or at the community kitchens outside that area. A meat dish can be obtained for about 4d. to 6d. and "afters" for about 2d. to 3d., tea for a penny, and children's portions half price. Find out now where these are from the Town Hall, Council offices or the Citizens' Advice Bureau in case of emergency.

THE INJURED

IF YOU are injured, treatment will be given at First Aid Posts and Hospitals, and :—

(a) If your doctor says you are unable to work as a result of a "war injury", you will be eligible to receive an *injury allowance*. Application should be made immediately to the local office of the Assistance Board and you should take with you, or send, a medical certificate from a doctor or a hospital.

(b) If you are afterwards found to be suffering from a serious and prolonged disablement, your case will be considered for a disability pension.

(c) Widows of workers and Civil Defence Volunteers killed on duty will receive £2 10s. 0d. a week for ten weeks, after which a widow's pension will become payable. Pensions for orphans and dependent parents are also provided.

Ask at the Post Office for the address of the local branch of the Ministry of Pensions if you want to apply for a pension.

KEEP THIS AND DO WHAT IT TELLS YOU. HELP IS WAITING FOR YOU. THE GOVERNMENT, YOUR FELLOW CITIZENS AND YOUR NEIGHBOURS WILL SEE THAT "FRONT LINE" FIGHTERS ARE LOOKED AFTER!

Issued by the Ministry of Home Security in co-operation with the following Departments: The Treasury, the Ministry of Health, the Ministry of Pensions the Ministry of Food and the Assistance Board

41—5415   10126: 12/40 D.L.

Every woman her own CLOTHES DOCTOR

NO NEED TO BE A SPECIALIST TO DEAL WITH THESE SIMPLE RENOVATIONS

Here are a few treatments for common clothes complaints—all quite easy to carry out and all well worth doing. Step-by-step instructions are given for some renovations—for others only the general idea is suggested which you can improve or adapt to your own needs.

TO LENGTHEN A DRESS

Let in a band of contrasting colour material (about the same weight) from the waist to 6 in. below and bind the neckline, add a pocket to match, or a contrasting band at the hem.

TO PREVENT A BAGGY SKIRT

Let out side seams if turnings allow. Half-line skirt to take strain—never lounge about in tailored skirt—ease slightly at hips before sitting down. Press often—hang when not in use.

Knickers Renewed

One good pair from two old pairs—here's how to manage it. Usually it is the gusset that's worn—so cut a new gusset from the good side of one pair (1) and take the old gusset out of the second pair (2). Diagrams 3, 4 and 5 show how to shape and join the new gusset, which should then be stitched into place. The raw edges should be cut down and blanket stitched (6) closely on the wrong side to make this as strong as possible.

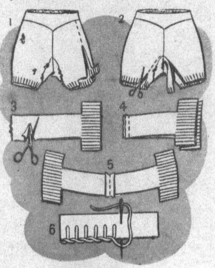

FRESHENING

WHEN mending or for, a great dea improving a garr and sponging and Grease spots are the mos —they can usually be go zinc powder over the m minutes and then shakin To make a success of pre press on the wrong side ex and if there is shine to cloth and hot iron, held the material. Shake or steam will penetrate wel hang at least a day bef that they may " set."

To keep a blouse within bounds

The blouse that won't stay put, inside a skirt; needs extra length— add a straight band of near-matching material, 3 in. wide, fixed

1 in. below waistline (A). Or crochet on a matching or contrasting band and wear it outside (B).

To give an old coat a fresh start

A shabby full-length coat can be smartened up simply by cutting it to the new hip length and using the extra material to make new collar and cuffs (if necessary) and a big patch pocket to hide a worn spot.

UP TACTICS

...-making is not called
...an be done towards
...t by removing stains
...essing with care.
...mmon cause of trouble
...ut by spreading a little
...s, leaving it for a few
...t off.
...ng, tack all pleats first :
...t for tailored garments;
...ove, use a very damp
...se but not actually on
...eat gently so that the
...Pressed clothes should
...being worn—in order

When a skirt tears where the pleats are
set in, work an arrowhead over the tear.
First strengthen with a piece of lining or
wide tape underneath. Then outline the
required shape with tacking. Begin working
at the bottom left-hand corner (A) ; take
a small stitch across the top, then a large
one at the bottom. Work top and bottom
alternately until the arrowhead is complete
(B).
Should the skirt already have an arrowhead
or the tear be too big for one, apply a cut
out motif in contrasting material to cover
the rent.

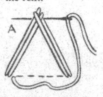

Decorative Elbow Patch

To make a really good
job of patching a frock
that's worn through at
the elbow, you will need
enough material for two
V-shaped strips—one for
each sleeve.
This material
can contrast
rather than
match, but if
so, try to introduce it some-
where else to bind collar and
pockets, say, or even to make a
bow for the neckline. Fold the
material as (A) and cut as shown.
Then stitch the strips on as (B).
The actual hole underneath
should be darned before
the patch is put on.

To renew worn gloves

Gloves are apt to " go " first at the under-
side of the fingertips or in the palms. If
small darns can no longer repair the
damage, unpick the good leather backs and
cut new undersides from thin felt or a firm
woollen fabric. Stitch together as before.

To keep pace with a growing girl

Last year's yoked frock
can be enlarged by un-
picking the skirt from
the yoke, dropping it
to waist level and in-
serting a contrasting
band to make the lower
part of the bodice. Use
bands of the same colour
to enlarge the sleeves.
The frock will still be
too tight across the chest
so insert a contrasting
band from the waistline
to the neck line.

Usually it is the base of the pocket that is worn. To repair, make a new half-pocket from strong bits from the piece bag. Join it to the old pocket half-way up, instead of unpicking the neat tailor's finish at the top opening.

When the sleeves of a jumper begin to show signs of wear at the elbows, take them out and change them over—left to right, right to left. They'll then last much longer. Also reinforce by darning over a piece of net.

The SHAPE of your dress

The appearance of a frock or suit is often spoilt by an ill-fitting corset. Great care should be taken to keep these trim and well repaired.

TO TAKE IN A BELT. A belt that has become too big for you because the rubber has perished, can be reshaped by making a strong seam down either side and down the centre of the back, or at the damaged point. Make the seam as flat as possible and cover with a piece of tape.

TO LET OUT A BELT. Unpick two side seams and insert a piece of strong material in each, machining and neatening as for the rest of the belt, or if more convenient, open centre back and insert a strip of strong material.

TO REPLACE CORSET ACCESSORIES. If the elastic on the suspenders of a new pair of corsets is too short, lengthen it before you wear the belt by adding a short piece of tape, otherwise you may tear your stockings. If you lose the back portion of a suspender remember that a small fabric-covered button padded on a length of tape can be used to take its place.

MENDING A CORSET. Corsets should be mended directly they need it. Never use a safety pin in a corset or suspender belt—it will pierce and break the rubber threads. If you need a patch, take this from the good parts of a discarded girdle; but if the damage is not too serious, use a darn over a piece of net.

(F.2817) Wt.53160 100,000 2/44 Gp.961 Fosh & Cross Ltd.   B.O.T.8.L.

IT'S THE GRUB THAT DOES THE DAMAGE

The great danger about moth is that you never know just when they are at their destructive work. For it is the hidden grubs, not the moths you see flying about, that do the damage. From September on into Spring, woollens, furs, bristles, hairstuffs and silk, if they are not in constant use and particularly if they are at all dirty, are in peril from these greedy pests. Always remember to—

WASH OR CLEAN BEFORE PUTTING AWAY

This applies to blankets and eiderdowns as well as to clothes— perfect cleanliness is a protection in itself. But if you are putting them " on the shelf " for some time, wrap them up in a snug newspaper parcel. The openings must be sealed with gummed paper. As an extra precaution the drawers and cupboards used for storage should be well scrubbed with carbolic or other disinfectant.

AIR OFTEN AND THOROUGHLY

This is another great safeguard. Moths hate being disturbed and you can keep them away by hanging clothes out at least once a month. Choose a fine, sunny day, brush everything well and hang in the open air. Heavy things can be beaten gently. Turn out pockets and look into every fold for eggs and grubs. Press the garment with a hot iron over a damp cloth, so that the steam penetrates the material.

Fighting Moth

IN WOOLLENS... IN CARPETS... IN UPHOLSTERY

Once the moth has got into your things, lose no time in dealing with the trouble —for moths work fast. Woollens and blankets should be hung outdoors for brushing and beating, then soaked for about one minute in water just too hot for the hands to bear— be careful not to change the temperature of the water or they will shrink. This will kill eggs and grubs. You can then wash in the ordinary way.

These must be taken up, underfelts as well, and hung outdoors. The boards should be well scrubbed with hot soapy water to which a disinfectant has been added. As an extra precaution or where the carpet cannot be hung out, the affected parts should be pressed with a very hot iron over a damp cloth.

If possible, move the affected furniture into the open air and leave it for several hours. Beat thoroughly. Should the infection be very bad, the coverings must be opened up and the padding sprayed with paraffin, very sparingly. Do not reclose the coverings for several days.

IN SILKS

Moth grubs may be found in silk through contact with other clothes that are moth-infected. To get rid of the grubs hang the clothes outdoors, then wash them in fairly hot water.

Another Danger

THE WOOLLY BEAR—*Watch out for small brown beetles known as Woolly Bears. They, too, can damage your belongings. Though not very common in this country they are sometimes seen in very hot linen cupboards. Like moths, they attack woollens, furs, blankets and bristles. Use the same methods for dealing with them as for getting rid of moths.*

Remember the moth **GRUB** is your real enemy

SUN, AIR AND CLEANLINESS ARE YOUR SAFEGUARDS...

Any further Questions ? ? ?

You may have some special moth worry which is not dealt with here. If so, go to your nearest Advice Centre for help or to a Make-do and Mend class where you can get a hand with repairs. The Citizen's Advice Bureaux will tell you about your nearest Advice Centre and Class.

(F.2867) Wt.56873 100,125 3/44 Gp.961 Fosh & Cross Ltd.

B.O.T.10 L.

CHILDREN'S UNDERWEAR BUYING AND REPAIR HINTS

"Keep them tidy underneath!"

says Mrs. SEW-and-SEW

It's quite a problem to keep children in underclothes. They give them such hard wear and grow out of them so quickly. Here are some practical hints which may help you keep them tidy underneath !

BUYING TIPS

★Never forget to allow for rapid growth. When buying ready-made underwear, always buy a size or more larger than needed.

When buying judge quality and workmanship by (*a*) well reinforced knicker forks and under-arms of vests. (*b*) good finish at edges of seams. These should be strong but soft to stand frequent washing and keep in shape, neither fraying nor chafing the skin. (*c*) Good button-hole finish and well-sewn seams.

ISSUED BY THE BOARD OF TRADE

WASHING HINTS

Careful washing prolongs the life of underclothes. If you're not quite sure of the correct methods it's worth while writing for Leaflet No. 5 on how to wash and care for woollies and Leaflet No. 6 on washing rayons.

KEEPING UP WITH THE GROWING CHILD

Here are some methods to make underclothes fit the child's present size.

TAKING IN. To shorten—put tucks at hemlines, turn up cuffs. To make waist narrower make small neat pleats. If you are making the clothes yourself, allow extra large turnings when you are cutting out.

LETTING OUT. This is not easy if the garments are ready-made, but still you can do a lot with the best parts of badly-worn underwear from your scrap-bag. For instance : to lengthen sleeves and legs—let down the hems and neaten with binding or facing. To lengthen pyjamas or pants—put in a deep belt at the waist. To enlarge magyar nightdresses add a deep yoke and sleeves. To alter nightdress sleeves which have become too short and tight—either cut to elbow length and re-hem, or add a deep cuff, or let in an extra strip of material, right up the seam to the armhole, and widen armhole. To widen tight yokes—let in inset pieces. This will also increase the size of the neckline.

REINFORCING DOUBLES WEAR

When reinforcing, these are the points that need attention—(a) forks of trousers and knickers. (b) Under-arms of sleeves, vests and shirts. (c) Toes and heels of socks and stockings. Darn on right side, using soft wool for woollen socks, and mending cotton for cotton and rayon. To reinforce hand-knit socks and stockings—knit double toes and heels. Also try to save enough wool for future reinforcements, mending and re-footing. You can get many useful hints from Leaflet No. 4.

MAKE FASTENINGS FAST!

When you first buy, it's a good idea to re-sew buttons, tapes and tie-strings with strong thread. To do away with broken buttonholes, stretch material and buttonhole over the end which takes the pull of the button. Stop torn openings on knickers, vests, nightdresses and pyjamas : stitch once or twice neatly over the end.

STITCH IN TIME!

Try to darn woollen underclothes before they wear into holes. It helps them to wear longer, and saves much labour. When snags and holes appear, be sure and patch with old pieces of the same material. Never use new material, or you will find it will tear away from the old. Leaflets No. 7 and No. 9 will tell you all about patching and darning.

After every wash, make a point of looking over all underwear and do the little that's needed every week. If underwear has been worn and repaired to give the greatest amount of wear, put it by. You will still be able to get one good garment out of 3 or 4 old ones. To do this cut a paper pattern from old garments before you cut away the best pieces. Put the good bits together, join them with flat seams, neat on both sides of the material. For stockinette cover turnings of joins with soft tape, and press pieces well before cutting out. Don't forget to save buttons, elastic, tape and edging for replacements for other made over garments.

MAKE DO'S

Old shirts, too far gone for further repairs, will make inside yoke linings for nightdresses, cotton frocks, linings for small boys' trousers, and half-linings for winter dresses. Pieces of old woven wear can be carefully joined to make excellent half-linings for rubber mackintoshes.

KNITTING PAYS!

★ Even an amateur can knit a child's vest, and you can always make a hand knitted garment bigger by knitting on to it. Or you can unpick it, and re-knit it a larger size by adding more wool. Try and buy an extra ounce of wool in the first place ; then you can enlarge the garment as the child grows.

MAKE DO AND MEND CLASSES OR ADVICE CENTRES

★ There are experts at these Classes and Centres who will give you every help with your sewing and coupon-saving renovations. Ask your Education Authority Evening Institute, Women's Organisation or Citizen's Advice Bureau where and when these Classes meet.

All leaflets mentioned here may be obtained free of charge from the Public Relations Department, Board of Trade, Millbank, S.W.1.

(56754) Wt. 59359/P5955 26-961-8 120,112 3/45 L. & B. B.O.T. 14 L

How to use
LARGE COKE
OR LARGE ANTHRACITE
in your boiler

Although the Battle for Fuel for the winter of 1942 is over, final victory on the coal front has not been won. Next winter our armies and industries will require still larger quantities of fuel, so there will be an even greater need to exercise the most rigid economy.

Transport for domestic fuel will become more difficult as next winter approaches, so now is the time to build up your reserves for the coming winter.

The Ministry of Fuel has restricted the amounts of house coal and sized fuels for boilers and stoves that any householder can accumulate without licence, but there are some fuels that at present are in better supply, and are available for the time being without restriction.

These are :—

Coke over $1\frac{1}{2}''$ in size, including 'Large' coke, and 'Broken or open fire' coke.
Anthracite over $1\frac{3}{8}''$ in size, including Anthracite cobbles, and Anthracite French nuts.

If you use these fuels in your house instead of the sizes that are in short supply, you can help the country and help yourself. You may have to use your ingenuity a little more to get the best out of these larger sized fuels, but here are a few tips to help you.

COKE AND ANTHRACITE FOR THE OPEN FIRE

The Ministry has already issued a leaflet telling you how to use the larger sizes of coke and anthracite mixed with coal on the open fire. Ask your merchant for a copy, and place an order now for some coke or anthracite of these sizes.

HOT WATER AND CENTRAL HEATING BOILERS

The normal sized fuels for the smaller units are coke or anthracite boiler nuts, but you will find that if you pay a little more attention to the boiler in the first place, you can use broken coke or anthracite French nuts satisfactorily. Even the bigger sizes, such as

large coke and anthracite cobbles, can be made to suit with the help of the coal hammer. The larger your hot water or central heating boiler is, the easier you will find it to burn these bigger sizes.

LIGHTING THE FIRE

It is a little more difficult to light your boiler fire with big fuel, and the best way to overcome this difficulty is to put some small pieces of house coal at the bottom. Or you can break the large coke

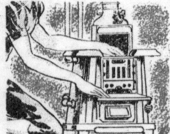

and anthracite and start the fire with the smaller pieces. If you have a separate supply of boiler nuts, then of course use that for lighting up, and keep the fire going with the bigger fuel.

KEEPING THE FIRE GOING

You may find that these larger sizes of coke and anthracite need somewhat different draught conditions than those ordinarily required. It is not a difficult matter to adjust your chimney dampers and your ashpit damper to suit the new conditions. Keep an eye on the fire for the first few days, and you will soon see just what amount of air is needed.

BANKING OVERNIGHT

It is difficult to keep the fire alight in smaller boilers overnight with large coke and anthracite. If you have a small stock of boiler nuts use them for banking and use the bigger pieces during the day. You probably keep two buckets by your boiler; fill one of them with boiler nuts and one with the larger fuel. Except in the coldest months, many families do not need their boiler running every day and night of the week, and they are particularly well able to help by using large coke or anthracite.

STOCKING COKE AND ANTHRACITE

Even if your coal consumption is small, you can still put down a stock of these larger sizes of coke and anthracite. They will come to no harm out of doors. The big pieces may break down a bit, but that will save you trouble with the coal hammer.

Always remember

NO ECONOMY IS TOO SMALL TO COUNT

Issued by the Ministry of Fuel and Power

Wt. 20779/P4054   50M   7/43   KJL/370/4   Gp.38/3

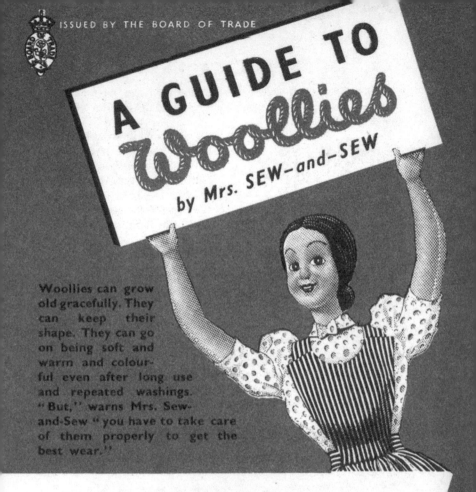

A GUIDE TO Woollies

by Mrs. SEW-and-SEW

Woollies can grow old gracefully. They can keep their shape. They can go on being soft and warm and colourful even after long use and repeated washings. "But," warns Mrs. Sew-and-Sew "you have to take care of them properly to get the best wear."

FIRST STEPS

If wool is not guaranteed pre-shrunk, wash skeins in fairly hot soap suds. Rinse thoroughly. Peg on clothes line away from heat or sun. Shake frequently while drying. Wind into loose balls so as not to strain wool.

TO JOIN WOOL

Join ends in wool by knotting at end of row, by knitting about 2 inches of new piece together with end of last piece or by darning end of last piece about 2 inches into new knitting with darning needle. Avoid knots in the middle of a row.

WILL IT FIT?

Most patterns say how many stitches and rows go to a square inch of knitting. You can change the size of the needles to increase or decrease the size.

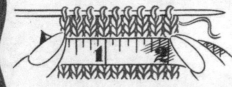

To wear and wash well, knitting should be smooth and even, close but not tight, elastic in texture. Vary size of needle and stitches to attain this standard. Shetland wool is an exception. Knit it in loose open stitches.

WILL IT WEAR?

Some parts always go first. Why not look ahead and knit toes and heels of socks, elbows of sleeves, with 2 strands of wool. Double wool means double life.

When knitting vests, knit welt on afterwards or knit down from shoulders to hem for ease in lengthening. Sleeves, too, can be knit from shoulder down to wrist so you can easily add new welts.

It is a good idea to run tapes down the seams of hand-knitted vests for extra strength. If the vest has only one side seam be sure to run a corresponding tape down the other side.

REINFORCEMENTS

FOR HAND KNITTEDS. Go over hand knitteds at regular intervals. If thin in places darn at once with fine wool on wrong side.

KNITTED PATCHES. If badly gone under the arms or at the elbows, you you can put in a strip of new knitting. Use a contrasting colour if you have no more of the original wool. It is not necessary to reknit the entire garment. Simply cut along

the last good row of knitting, after unpicking the nearby seams. Unravel the worn parts and run a fine knitting needle through the upper loops. Knit in the patch on the lower stitches and graft the last row of the patch on to the stitches on the fine needle.

ADDED STRENGTH FOR MACHINE KNITS

Machine knits last longer when reinforced in the places that get most wear. It's a good idea to patch in pieces of old soft underwear at the back of neck of men's vests, under arms, in the fork of pants or girls' knickers. Herringbone stitch in place. Make small stiches but keep sewing loose.

Re-sew buttons. Put a stitch or two across ends of button holes to prevent fraying and help them keep in shape.

Put a little patch of soft silk under pocket corners on the wrong side to prevent stretching. Machine pocket corners down over existing stitches. Darn elbows on wrong side for extra strength.

SPECIAL TIPS *for* HOME KNITTERS

A one plain, one purl single rib is better for boys' wear than stocking stitch.

If possible, use new wool for the welt even when you are re-knitting old wool for the body of the garment. Old wool hasn't enough elasticity for a firm welt.

When casting on, put needle behind instead of through stitches. This makes a firm edge so that there is no need to knit into back of stitches in first row.

Graft rather than knit 2 rows together when finishing off toes of socks. With right side of work towards you break off wool, leaving 12". Thread through a darning needle. Hold knitting needles parallel and thread the darning needle through the first stitch on front needle as if you were to knit the stitch, and draw it off the needle, now thread the darning needle purlwise through second stitch of the front needle, but leave it on needle. Bring the thread round under the front needle to the back needle and repeat process until all the stitches have been slipped off. Darn in thread at end. For hard wear, cast off sleeve welts within 2 strands of wool. Recommended for boys' jerseys.

MAKE-DO'S FOR WOOLLEN GARMENTS

Worn, faded, and out of shape hand knitteds can be reknitted if care is taken in the unpicking and washing of the unravelled wool. There are several points to remember.

1 Unpick the seams carefully—see you don't snip the knitted stitches.

2 Unravel the knitting, winding the wool round a tray or lid of a dress box.

3 Tie the skeins in several places before taking it off the tray or box lid.

4 Dip the skeins up and down in warm suds, this will remove the dirt and the crinkles. If the wool is very dirty swish gently without tangling, rinse very carefully and thoroughly.

5 Dry the skeins by stringing them on a line and pegging them up to two spaced hooks, or over a clothes line. Shake the skeins occasionally to prevent tangling and matting.

6 Wind loosely into balls, sort the skeins, keeping those with the fewest knots for the largest pieces of knit-ting. Remember that re-knitting always means a smaller knitted article, such as a jumper from a cardigan, or short sleeves where there were long ones. Before you start re-knitting it is a good idea to weigh the wool and reckon an ounce less to account for the frayed strands and broken ends. When choosing your pattern for re-knitting avoid an open-work one as it is difficult to hide joins successfully in the middle of a row. When you join the ends of the wool see that the join comes inside your new jumper, or whatever you are knitting or at the beginning of a row. The ends can be darned in loosely after the knitting has been pressed.

TO WASH WOOLLIES

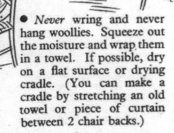

● Use plenty of warm suds. Put a tablespoon of household ammonia in the water. Keep woollies under the surface while washing. Squeeze suds through them. Don't rub except for very dirty spots. Rinse in plenty of water about the same temperature as washing water.

● *Never* wring and never hang woollies. Squeeze out the moisture and wrap them in a towel. If possible, dry on a flat surface or drying cradle. (You can make a cradle by stretching an old towel or piece of curtain between 2 chair backs.)

● Shake frequently while drying and pull woollies into shape when you turn them about. Before washing a new garment, it is a good idea to measure it and whilst drying it to pull it to these measurements. Run a tacking thread through neck, wrist and waist welts before washing to keep size. Don't try to remove stains from infants' woollen frocks or knitted pilches. Frequent washing is best, as some stain removers destroy wool, and remember, dry your woollies wrong side out.

HOW TO STORE WOOLLIES

Always wash woollies before putting them away. Roll up in clean paper with some flaked napthalene and seal the parcel up.

F4359 Wt. 52911 120,000 3/45 Gp. 961 Fosh & Cross Ltd.   B.O.T. 15L.

Save Fuel for Battle

WHY TO SAVE Coal is essential to our advancing forces. Your fuel savings in the home will help to keep them supplied.

WHAT TO SAVE Over two-thirds of the fuel most of us use in our homes is burnt as raw coal. Thus whilst we must economize in the use of gas, coke, and electricity which also come from coal, *the biggest saving must be made on raw coal.*

WHERE TO SAVE MOST Roughly half our fuel is used for room heating and one quarter for water heating, i.e., three-quarters for these two purposes alone. Therefore *we must cut down on room heating and water heating.*

WHEN TO SAVE Nearly half our fuel is used in the three coldest months, December, January and February, but do *remember that big savings can be made in the mild and less cold weather.*

HOW TO SAVE *Most households following the simple hints given in this folder can save at least 5 lbs. coal per day without much discomfort.* This does not sound very much, but see on the back of this folder what it means to our fighting men, and start in real earnest to economize *now.*

Room Heating

Half our fuel is used for room heating. You should start heating rooms *late* in the season and finish heating rooms *early* in the season. Similarly start heating rooms *late* in the day and finish heating rooms *early* in the day. Wear warmer clothes indoors—coatees, pullovers, dressing gowns can all be pressed into service. Try to arrange to have only one room in the house heated : whenever possible make the kitchen your living room. Stop all draughts.

THE OPEN FIRE

1. Firebricks can save 15% to 20% (equivalent to ½lb. coal per hour). Replenish a bright fire with *coke* or *anthracite.*

2. Yesterday's cinders mixed with coal, will help to light to-day's fire. Approximately ½ lb. to 1 lb. of cinders can be saved and used again in the average household.

3. Don't use the poker for the sake of a blaze. An unbroken lump of coal burns far longer than the same lump broken into pieces.

4. When the room is warm, or whenever it is left unoccupied, bank the fire with moistened slack, tea leaves or cinders.

5. Do without that last shovel of coal near bed-time.

6. Before you retire, spread the fire to die out quickly and you will have good cinders for to-morrow's fire.

COKE GRATES

1. If you light the fire with gas, a few bits of wood will mean a big saving of gas.

2. A little coal mixed with the coke will get the fire going quicker.

3. Don't poke at the top and disturb the surface. Clear the ash gently from below.

4. Don't let the ash-pan fill up and choke the grate bars.

5. Don't let the fire get too low or you'll waste fuel in replenishing. A " blower " saves using gas.

COMBINATION GRATES

1. Keep two buckets by the grate, one with coal, one with slack.

2. Consider carefully where heat is most required, i.e., for cooking, warming room, heating water.

3. If you don't need more hot water, cover flue with slack and close the damper. If not cooking, cover oven flue with slack.

4. Have a hot fire near the flue you need, but cover top with small coal to keep cold air away from it.

5. Keep all flues clean and swept.

GAS FIRES

1. Never light unless really necessary. Turn on late in the day, turn off early in the evening.

2. Turn down the gas as soon as the room is warm enough ; a smaller fire will keep it warm.

3. Turn out the fire if the room is to be left empty for any length of time.

4. Don't use a gas fire in preference to solid fuel fires during the coldest weather (December to March) when the demand for gas is very heavy. In milder weather a small portable gas fire saves coal. For short period heating, a large gas fire saves coal.

HEATING STOVES

1. Stoves are economical only if they are kept closed. Never open the front doors except for fuelling. Keep the ash-pit door closed.

2. See that the sealing plate snugly fits the chimney opening or warm air will escape and soot will give trouble. Seal up air-leaks and replace cracked mica.

3. Many stoves can also be used for heating saucepans and kettles.

4. Use the fuel the maker recommends. If your coal merchant can't supply it, ask for the best alternative.

5. Never let the fire burn fiercely ; it wastes fuel and may damage the stove.

FIREBRICKS CAN SAVE ½ LB OF COAL AN HOUR
HAVE YOU FITTED THEM IN **YOUR** GRATE ?

ELECTRIC FIRES

1. Don't switch on an electric fire—*especially between 8 a.m. and 1 p.m.*—unless absolutely necessary. NEVER switch on an electric fire because it happens to be handy, easy or attractive.

2. Electric heaters should not be used in preference to solid fuel fires during the coldest weather (December to March) when the demand for electricity is very heavy.

3. Don't use two bars when one will do ; better still, never use two bars.

4. Electric fires should not be used to heat halls, staircases or landings. Only in case of emergency should you use them in bedrooms.

5. An electric fire should never be left switched on in an unoccupied room.

6. In milder weather small electric fires give all the heat you want and save coal.

7. For short period heating, large electric fires also save coal.

Water Heating

Hot water, so abundant for all domestic purposes in peace-time, must now be regarded as a definite luxury. Countless gallons of hot water can be thoughtlessly wasted unless you exercise care and economy every moment of the day. Use less water for *all purposes* and never wash under a running tap. Except when hot water is required for weekly bath it is more economical to heat small quantities in kettles. NEVER use MORE than 5 INCHES of water in your weekly bath. Finally, wrap up or lag all tanks and pipes. This will conserve the heat.

HOT WATER BOILERS

1. Don't roar the fire. Control it by means of dampers.

2. Except in the coldest weather when the independent boiler is used to warm the house, it should not be used to heat water more than twice a week.

3. Keep a small bright fire and see that it burns right to the back which heats the water quickest.

4. Rake out the ash *from below* with the boiler rake. You will keep up far more heat this way.

5. Don't burn rubbish ; save it for salvage.

GAS & ELECTRIC WATER HEATERS

Keep electric water heaters *switched off* during the daytime and particularly between 8 a.m. and 1 p.m. and heat the water at night.

Turn out the pilot lights of gas water heaters at night, unless you are very short of matches.

5" OF WATER IS AMPLE FOR A WAR-TIME BATH
HAVE YOU MADE THIS **YOUR** RULE ?

Cooking

Do not use the oven for a single dish. Use it to capacity by cooking something else at the same time, for example a casserole stew that can be re-heated, a milk pudding or fruit pie that can be eaten cold. Don't boil three pints of water when you need only two. Always remember to use wide vessels and to keep the lids on. Don't keep opening oven door. When boiling vegetables, use as little water as possible. Always keep the hot plates and the outside of kettles and pans clean and see that heat reaches them.

COAL COOKERS 1. Even after the fire has died down, you can often do slow cooking in the oven or heat water in it.
2. Fit fire bricks where possible. Never let the fire roar. Use up all cinders.
3. The makers are experts in fuel economy—follow their instructions whenever you can.

GAS COOKERS 1. Always use a small ring if you can. It may take a little longer but it saves gas.
2. Turn off the burners before removing vessel. Never let gas flare round a vessel.
3. Turn down the gas under a saucepan as soon as the contents boil ; a very small flame will keep them boiling.
4. Use grill as little as possible.

ELECTRIC COOKERS 1. Watch the oven thermometer ; immediately the required temperature is reached switch to " low."
2. Switch off before the food is quite cooked. The electric oven will retain heat which can be used for simmering or heating water.
3. Whenever possible, make sure the hot plate is fully covered. It is often possible to boil two saucepans on one hot plate.
4. Use residual heat on hot plate for warming washing-up water.
5. Turn the main control switch off immediately the cooker is finished with.
6. It is more economical to use an electric kettle than to boil an ordinary kettle on an electric hot-plate.

READ THESE AMAZING FIGURES

Do you know that one single family reducing fuel consumption by the equivalent in gas, coal or electricity of 5 lbs. of coal per day during the thirty weeks of colder weather would save enough fuel to produce

2,000 More Cartridges and Bullets	2 More twenty-five pounder Shells
3 More Sten Guns	10 More Rifles

If EVERY family did the same it would mean all the following :

1,000 More Heavy Bombers	1,250,000 More Rifles
5,000 More Spitfires	5,000,000 More 6 in. Shells
5,000 More 6 in. Guns	500,000,000 More Cartridges
5,000 More Light Tanks	

FUEL SAVING   FOR VICTORY

ISSUED BY THE MINISTRY  **OF FUEL & POWER**

Printed by Fosh & Cross Ltd., London.   51-4322

CLOTHING COUPON

QUIZ

Answers to Questions on the Rationing of Clothing, Footwear, Cloth and Knitting Yarn

Issued by the Board of Trade
and published by
His Majesty's Stationery Office

**Price 2d. net or
3s. net for 25 copies**

Subject Index

For list of coupon values see paragraphs 9, 10, 11, 12, 13 and 14.

HOW

the Rationing Scheme works

1. There is enough for all if we share and share alike. Rationing is the way to get fair shares. *Fair shares*—when workers are producing guns, aeroplanes and bombs instead of frocks, suits and shoes. *Fair shares*—when ships must run the gauntlet with munitions and food rather than with wool and cotton. *Fair shares*—when movements of population outrun local supplies. It is *your* scheme—to defend you as a consumer and as a citizen. All honest people realise that trying to beat the ration is the same as trying to cheat the nation.

2. You must present coupons to buy clothing, cloth, footwear and knitting yarn. The coupons to be used first are the "Margarine" Coupons in your Food Ration Book issued in January, 1941. There are 26 coupons on the margarine page, and the numbers printed on them are to be ignored ; each coupon counts 1 only.

3. You do not have to use up all the margarine coupons in your old Food Book by any particular date. It is much better to keep your coupons as long as possible—you should plan your needs, looking ahead a little.

4. When you have used the coupons in your old Food Book you will have to take this Book to the Post Office and exchange it for one of the new Clothing Cards with 40 coupons, making a total of 66 coupons for the full year (ending 31st May, 1942). Coupons for clothing can be used in any quantity at any time, except that when you get your new Clothing Card you will find on it 20 coupons marked X. These can only be used after 1st January, 1942. Keep your old Food Book in safety until you have used all the margarine coupons ; you can then exchange it for a Clothing Card.

5. Use your coupons for whatever clothing you need—*when* you need it. You can shop anywhere without registration—the retailer will simply cut out the proper number of margarine coupons from your Food Book and give it back to you. *Do not cut the coupons out yourself.* (It is illegal to sell or buy coupons, for this would defeat the purpose of "*fair shares.*")

6. If you order goods by post, however, you must cut out the correct number of coupons yourself, sign your name clearly on the back, and send them with the order. If the retailer cannot supply you, you can either let him keep the coupons and order something else, or you can have them sent back. If you get them back they can only be used for another order by post. They will not be accepted over the counter.

7. Special cases are being looked after. Expectant mothers get a special ration to cover the baby clothes, and there is a list of infants' clothes (suitable for the "under fours") which require very few coupons. Because children grow fast their clothes are rated at less coupons than grown peoples', provided they wear clothes of types and sizes which are exempt from Purchase Tax. Children who are too big to wear these clothes will be given extra coupons. The details of this scheme will be announced later. People who have been bombed out are able to get special replacement coupons for essential clothing.

8. What Clothing Coupons look like

Illustrations of the coupons for clothing are shown here for your guidance. The examples depict single coupons, but your coupons must not be cut from the Food Book or Clothing Card by anyone except the retailer. The actual coupons you use have tinted patterned backgrounds, whilst the coupon vouchers (*d*, *e* and *f*), issued for special cases, are printed on tinted paper.

(*a*) shows the " margarine " coupons from your old Food Book. (*The " Butter and Margarine " coupons from the Ration Book you have for food for the period commencing July*, 1941, *are NOT valid for clothing*) ;

(a)

(*b*) and (*c*) depict the coupons on the Clothing Cards which are now ready for issue (see para. 56) ;

(*d*), (*e*) and (*f*) are emergency vouchers issued in 10's, 5's and 2's to people who need them for special reasons, such as the replacement of essential clothing after being bombed out.

(b)

(c)

(d)

(e)

(f)

9. Number of coupons needed for the principal articles of adults' and children's clothing

The following table sets out the number of coupons needed for various articles of clothing, other than infants' clothing dealt with on pages vii and viii. The figures in the last column apply to types and sizes which are exempt from Purchase Tax, and depend on the size of the garment—not on the age of the child.

"Woollen" in relation to any rationed goods means containing more than 15 per cent. by weight of wool. "Fur" includes imitation fur.	Man	Woman	*Child

Overcoat, Raincoat, etc.

	Man	Woman	*Child
¶ Mackintosh, raincoat, overcoat, cape, cloak—			
(a) if unlined or saddle-lined, and not woollen, leather, fur or double-texture	9	9	7
(b) if fully-lined and woollen, leather or fur	18	18	11
(c) other than those in (a) and (b)	16	15	10
Overcoat lining (detached)	7	7	4

Jacket, Cardigan, Waistcoat or Pullover

	Man	Woman	*Child
§ Jacket, blouse-type jacket, long-sleeved waistcoat, coat, blazer, woman's cape, woman's bolero—			
(a) if lined, and woollen or leather or fur	13	12	8
(b) if unlined and not woollen, leather, fur or double-texture	6	6	4
(c) if unlined, blouse-type and knitted		8	
(d) other than those in (a). (b) or (c)	10	10	6
‡ Bolero, short jacket, short cape—			
(a) if woollen or leather, and with sleeves of not less than elbow length		5	
(b) if not woollen or leather, and with no sleeves or with sleeves of less than elbow length		2	
(c) other than those in (a) or (b)		3	
Cardigan, sweater, jersey, jumper, pullover, bedjacket—woollen and weighing at least 10 ozs. (7 ozs. for children)	8	8	5
Cotton football jersey	4		2
Waistcoat, pullover, jumper, jersey, sweater, cardigan, bedjacket—other than those described above	5	5	3

Trousers, Shorts or Skirt

	Man	Woman	*Child
Trousers, slacks, over-trousers, breeches, jodhpurs—if woollen ; kilt	8	8	6
Trousers, slacks, over-trousers, breeches, jodhpurs—not woollen	5	5	4
Shorts—if woollen	5	5	3
Shorts—not woollen	3	3	2
Skirt, divided skirt—if woollen		6	4
Skirt, divided skirt—not woollen		4	3

* Types and sizes exempt from Purchase Tax, including protective boots, but not children's garments containing silk or fur.
¶ Women's coats and capes fall into one of these categories if over 28 in. long.
§ Women's coats, capes and jackets fall into one of these categories if over 16 in. but not over 28 in. long · also fur jackets even if not over 16 in. long.
‡ Not over 16 in. long, and not fur.

Continued on next page

	Man	Woman	Child
Dress, Gown, Frock or Gym Tunic			
Dress, gown, frock—if woollen and with sleeves of any length ..		11	8
Dress, gown, frock—not woollen		7	5
Gym tunic, skirt on bodice, sleeveless frock—woollen		8	6
Gym tunic, skirt on bodice—not woollen		6	4
Shirt, Blouse or Shawl			
Shirt†—if woollen	7		6
Shirt†—not woollen	5		4
Blouse, shirt-blouse, shawl, plaid—if woollen		6	4
Blouse, shirt-blouse, shawl, plaid—not woollen		4	3
Blousette		2	1
Miscellaneous Garments			
One-piece shelter suit or like garment	11	11	8
Cassock—if woollen	8		6
Cassock—not woollen	7		5
Overall, Apron or Housecoat			
Apron (with or without bib)	3	3	2
Overall—if woollen	11	11	8
Sleeveless non-woollen overall		6	4
Overall—other than above	7	7	5
Housecoat—if woollen		8	
Housecoat—not woollen		7	
Dressing-Gown, Pyjamas, Nightdress, etc.			
Dressing-gown—if woollen	8	8	6
Dressing-gown—not woollen	7	7	5
Pyjama suit, nightshirt	8	8	6
Nightdress		6	5
Undergarments, etc.			
Combinations, petticoat—if woollen	7	6	4
Combinations, petticoat—not woollen; slip, corselette	5	4	3
Suspender belt (not more than 10 in. in width at widest part), brassiere, bust bodice, modesty vest		1	1
Woollen vest; non-woollen vest with sleeves of any length; woollen pants or trunks; non-woollen pants (long legs) ..	4	3	2
Body-belt,§ non-woollen briefs (no legs), camisole	2	2	2
Undergarment not elsewhere listed; athlete's vest	3	3	2
Stockings, Socks, Collar, Tie, Handkerchief, etc.			
Pair of non-woollen half-hose, woman's ankle-socks	1	1	1
Pair of other socks, or stockings	3	2	1
Collar, shirt-front,† pair of cuffs, tie—of masculine type.. ..	1	1	1
4 small handkerchiefs (each of area less than 1 sq. ft.), pair of sleeves	1	1	1
2 large handkerchiefs not more than 2 ft. in length or breadth ..	1	1	1
Bathing Costume, Bathing Gown, etc.			
Bathing gown—if woollen	8	8	6
Bathing gown—not woollen	7	7	5
Bathing costume	3	3	2
Woollen bathing trunks	3		1
Cotton swimming drawers	1		1

* Types and sizes exempt from Purchase Tax, including protective boots, but not children's garments containing silk or fur.   † With or without collar attached.   § Knitted or woven body-belt without fastening and without reinforcement by means of elastic, boning or inner lining.

Continued on next page

		Man	Woman	* Child

Footwear, Leggings, etc.

Description	Man	Woman	Child
Pair of goloshes, rubber overshoes, rubber bootees, plimsolls,† man's slippers, woman's heelless bedroom slippers, football boots, hockey boots or shoes, lacrosse boots or shoes, running shoes, race walking shoes or boots, boxing boots, cycling shoes or bowls shoes	4	4	2
Pair of sandals or rubber-soled canvas shoes other than those listed above	5	5	2
Pair of boots, bootees, shoes, overshoes, overboots, woman's slippers, or footwear not described above (including cricket and golf)	7	5	2
Pair of leggings, gaiters or spats	3	3	2

Gloves, Scarf or Fur Garments

Description	Man	Woman	Child
Scarf or sash—over 5¼ sq. ft. ; pair of gloves or mittens—containing leather or fur ; muff (other than fur)	2	2	2
Scarf or sash—not over 5¼ sq. ft. ; pair of gloves or mittens—not containing leather or fur	1	1	1
Fur cape,‡ fur stole or tie (other than fox), fur collar, fur muff (not over 12 in. length or breadth), pair of fur cuffs ..		5	
Fox fur stole or tie, mounted or unmounted .. *per skin*		5	

* Types and sizes exempt from Purchase Tax, including protective boots, but not children's garments containing silk or fur.   † See para. 40.   ‡ Not over 16 in. long.

10. Number of coupons needed for articles of infants' clothing

Items not on this list, such as scarves, handkerchiefs, and gloves, have the same rating as for children. " Woollen " in relation to any rationed goods means containing more than 15 per cent. by weight of wool. " Fur " includes imitation fur.

Description of Garment "l." indicates "length"	Coupons needed	Maximum measurements "l." indicates "length"
Overcoat, raincoat, mackintosh, cape— (a) fully lined and woollen or fur .. .. .. (b) unlined or saddle-lined and not woollen or fur .. (c) other than those in (a) or (b)	 6 4 5	*Overcoat :* 22″ l. from centre back collar seam to hem. *Other items :* 26″ length from centre back collar seam to hem.
Infants' shawl over 4 ozs. ..	4	
Coat or cape—not over 16″ l. ; Infants' shawl not over 4 ozs.	2	
Jacket, blazer, or like garment.	4	26″ chest.

Continued on next page

Description of Garment "l." indicates "length"	Coupons needed	Maximum measurements "l." indicates "length"
Matinee coat, cardigan, jersey, jumper, blouse— (a) over 12" l. .. .. (b) not over 12" l.	 2 1	*Cardigan :* 16" l.,§ and 24" chest.† *Blouse :* 14" length.§ *Other items :* 18" length,§ and 24" chest.
Boy's shorts (other than fully-lined), leggings with feet .. Leggingettes, pantettes, gaiter overalls, breechettes, fully-lined shorts	 1 2	*Shorts :* 23" from top of waist (centre front) to crutch and thence to top of waist (centre back). *Other garments :* 26" overall l. along outer side seam.
Pair of gaiters	1	18" overall l. along outer side seam.
Skirt on bodice, kilt on bodice.	2	22" l. (centre shoulder to skirt hem).
Frock, pinafore frock, overall, buster suit, or like garment; baby's day-gown, baby's nightgown— (a) if woollen .. .. (b) not woollen	 3 2	*Frock, pinafore frock or frock overall :* 22" l. from centre shoulder seam at front to hem. *Buster suit or like garment :* 22" length from centre shoulder seam or strap to full length of garment when buttoned. *Trouser overalls :* 36" length.§
Dressing - gown, one-piece shelter suit, or like garment	4	*Dressing gown :* 33" l. from centre back collar seam to hem. *Shelter suit or like garment :* 38" length.§
Pyjama suit, sleeping-suit, nightdress— (a) if woollen .. .. (b) not woollen	 4 3	*Pyjama suit :* 26" outside l. of pyjama leg (waist to bottom of leg). *Sleeping suit :* 36" l. from centre back collar seam to hem. *Nightdress :* 33" length.§
Combinations, short petticoat, long petticoat, long flannel ..	2	*Combinations or short petticoat :* 22" l. from centre shoulder strap or seam to full length of garment.
Bodice, vest, trunks, knickers for underwear (inc. waterproof knickers), napkin. (*Napkins of muslin are exempt, as is the material.*)	1	*Bodice :* 15" length.§ *Vest :* 22" length§ and 22" chest.† *Trunks or knickers :* 23" from top of waist (centre front) to crutch and thence to top of waist (centre back).
Pair of socks or knitted bootees	⅓rd.	*Socks :* 7" foot l. from heel to point of toe.
Pair of boots, shoes, overshoes, sandals or slippers	1	Size 9 or smaller.
Infant's bib or feeder ; pair of infantees ; wrapper vest, body belt, knitted binder, pilch ..	⅓rd.	

† In the case of chest measurements the garment should be buttoned (if it has buttons) and measured across chest (1" below armpit), this figure being multiplied by two.
§ From centre shoulder seam to hem.

11. Cloth

Single-texture Cloth, Ribbon and Elastic over 3 in. in width.

Width of Cloth.*	Woollen.	Other.
	Coupons required per yard.	
Over 3 in. and not over 9 in.	$\frac{1}{2}$	$\frac{1}{3}$
„ 9 „ „ „ 15 „	1	$\frac{2}{3}$
„ 15 „ „ „ 21 „	$1\frac{1}{2}$	1
„ 21 „ „ „ 27 „	2	$1\frac{1}{3}$
„ 27 „ „ „ 33 „	$2\frac{1}{4}$	$1\frac{2}{3}$
„ 33 „ „ „ 39 „	3	2
„ 39 „ „ „ 45 „	$3\frac{1}{2}$	$2\frac{1}{4}$
„ 45 „ „ „ 51 „	4	$2\frac{2}{3}$
„ 51 „ „ „ 57 „	$4\frac{1}{2}$	3
And for every 6 in. or part thereof in excess of 57 in.	$\frac{1}{2}$	$\frac{1}{3}$
Fents (or remnants)†	4 per lb.	

* The number of coupons needed for double and multiple texture cloth is the sum of the numbers of coupons specified in respect of the component cloths.
† Fents (or remnants) are lengths of fabrics (usually the ends of pieces) which are too short to be sold at full price, and which it is customary to sell by weight in the wholesale trade. In the retail trade the fent (or remnant) should not exceed $2\frac{1}{2}$ yards in length for fabrics not exceeding 36 in. in width, or $1\frac{1}{2}$ yards in length for fabrics exceeding 36 ins. in width. Remnants should not be sold as fents unless they are sold by weight and at least two lengths of fabrics are sold together.

12. Knitting Yarn

The number of coupons required for hand-knitting yarn containing more than 16 per cent. by weight of wool is one coupon for every 2 ounces.

13. Coupon-free Articles

Abdominal belts specially designed solely for use in the following conditions : hernia, sacroiliac disease, spinal abnormality and enuresis.

Abdominal belts specially designed for post-operative use, the following : (1) supra pubic drainage belts ; (2) colotomy belts ; (3) belts for appendicectomy ; (4) belts for nephrectomy.

Ankle supports.

Anti-scatter fabrics.

Apparel made of paper or feathers.

Aprons made wholly of rubber.

Ballet shoes.

Belts (except underwear).

Bias binding.

Black-out material of cotton which complies with the ‡British Standard Specification BSI/ARP/23, being either :

a. dyed all black, and of any weight ; or

b. of plain or twill weave dyed dark blue, dark brown or dark green, and weighing not less than 7 ozs. per square yard.

Boot and shoe laces.

Braces, garters and suspenders.

Carpets, carpeting, matting and other floor cloth.

Clogs.

Cloth either sensitized or specially prepared for photo-mechanical reproduction.

Cloth (including ribbon and elastic) not over 3 inches in width.

Cloth of any width of the following descriptions as defined in the §War Emergency British Standard Miscellaneous Definitions BS/983–1941 : *American cloth, bolting cloth, book muslin, buckram, butter muslin, canvas, cheese cloth, gauze muslin, leather cloth, leno, lint, mull, scrim, tarlatan.*

‡§ BSI/ARP/23 (price 4d. post free), and BS/982–1941 and BS/983–1941 (published together price 1s. 3d. post free) are obtainable from the British Standards Institution, 28 Victoria Street, London, S.W.1.

*Cloth of the following descriptions exceeding 12 inches in width :
(1) Figured jacquard woven fabrics, being brocade, brocatelle, damask, jacquard repp, tapestry, needlework tapestry or hand needlework tapestry, tissue, matelasse, folk weave, figured casement ;
(2) Pile fabrics, being genoa velvet, mohair velvet, terry velvet, moquette, plush ;
(3) Plain fabrics, being chenille, repp, Roman satin ;
(4) Printed fabrics weighing not less than 7 ounces per square yard, being printed cretonne, printed chintz, printed linen, printed crash, printed union ;
(defined in the †War Emergency British Standard Definitions of Furnishing Fabrics BS/982–1941).

Cloth other than woollen weighing more than 15 ounces per square yard, including rubber-proofed sheeting.

Dress shields.

Emery cloth, and insulation cloth.

Filter cloth.

Garments of asbestos and garments specially designed for protection against poison gas.

Glass replacement fabric.

Gloves made wholly of rubber; household gloves of undressed leather and sports gloves.

Hard haberdashery.

Headgear other than that made from scarves or incorporating handkerchiefs.

Holland.

Jock straps.

Knee caps.

Lace, lace net, and curtain net.

Linen cloth weighing more than 15 ounces per square yard.

Mending yarn, made up in skeins or on cards, in quantities not exceeding ¼ ounce in weight and of a yarn count not exceeding three-fold 20's.

Oiled silk, oiled cambric, and jaconet, if sold in lengths not exceeding 45 inches.

Oiled wool (as defined in †BS/983–1941).

Overalls of the following descriptions : *Unlined trouser overalls (including boiler suits and bib and brace overalls) of plain or twill weave cotton material, in plain single colour, being of a type made for use in the course of their trade or occupations by artisans.*

Sanitary belts, sanitary knickers, sanitary towels.

Shin guards and leg guards.

Surgical bandages.

Surgical elastic stockings, knee caps and ankle supports ; stump socks.

Tracing cloth.

* These furnishing fabrics are only coupon-free in sales to retail customers ; coupons must be surrendered in sales between traders, unless these sales are made under licence.
† BS/982–1941 and BS/983–1941 are published together by the British Standards Institution, 28 Victoria Street, London, S.W.1, price 1s. 3d. post free.

14. Secondhand articles

(See also paragraph 65)

Secondhand goods require coupons if sold above fixed prices. These prices are fixed by multiplying the number of coupons that would be required for the article if new by the price given in the list below.

	s.	d.
(1) Hand-knitting yarn, cloth and stockings and woollen socks for men and boys		8
(2) Undergarments, stockings and socks other than those in the preceding item	1	0
(3) Boots, bootees, shoes, overshoes, slippers and sandals	1	6
(4) Other rationed goods	2	0

If sold above these prices rationed goods, even though genuinely secondhand, will require the full number of coupons.

Your questions answered

USE THE SUBJECT INDEX ON PAGE ii.

15. Where and when can I use my Ration Book or Clothing Card? The coupons may be used at any shop or number of shops. They may be used at any rate and at any time except for 20 out of the 40 on the Clothing Card, which will be found to be marked X and which can only be used after 1st January, 1942. The object of this is to even out the demand.

16. Are clothes of sizes suitable for babies under four rationed now? Yes, the coupon ratings are given in paragraph 10.

17. How can men in the Services obtain clothing? The following articles of uniform may be supplied without coupons to Officers and Cadets of the Navy, Army and Air Force (including the W.R.N.S., A.T.S. and W.A.A.F.) and of the Allied Forces. These goods may also be supplied without coupons by one trader to another:—

Tunics, naval jackets and trousers, Service dress; tunics, naval jackets and trousers of khaki or white drill; skirts (when sold with tunic); greatcoats; breeches of khaki drill (when sold with tunic); shorts of khaki drill (when sold with tunic).

Officers and Cadets who are serving members of H.M. Forces, when purchasing other rationed goods, and officers of the Naval, Military and Air Force Nursing Services, when purchasing rationed goods, including articles of uniform, may for the time being obtain supplies of rationed goods by signing a statement on the back of the trader's bill that the articles mentioned represent their essential personal requirements. The rank and regiment or unit should be indicated. Officers of the R.A.F. should sign with their name, rank and personal number only. Newly commissioned officers should show the shopkeeper their calling-up papers as proof of identity.

Only Officers and Cadets who are serving members of H.M. Forces and who do not possess civilian clothing coupons may sign bills in this way. A.T.C. Officers may sign for personal *uniform* requirements only. No other Officers or Cadets may sign.

Chief and Petty Officers of the Navy, Warrant Officers of the Army and Air Force, non-commissioned officers, ratings, and other ranks of all the Services mentioned may obtain similar facilities provided that a document is attached to the bill, signed by their commanding officer (or by the officer duly authorised to act on his behalf) and testifying that the goods represent essential personal requirements of types not supplied to them by the authorities.

The statements of certificate must in all cases be signed by the officers mentioned above. Delegation of authority to sign is not permitted.

18. If I want a dress made, do I have to give up the same number of coupons whatever the amount of cloth needed may be? If you first buy the cloth and then give it back to be made up, you surrender coupons according to the yardage. If you arrange to buy the dress when it has been made, then you give 11 coupons if it is woollen and 7 if it is of other material.

19. For how long will current year coupons be valid? Both the " margarine " and Clothing Card coupons are valid at least up to 31st May, 1942.

20. What about woollen mixtures : how are they rated? Garments containing more than 15 per cent. by weight of wool are graded as " wool." This means that nearly all mixtures containing wool count as " woollen."

21. Are coupons required for knitting yarn? Yes, provided it contains more than 16 per cent. by weight of wool. " Wool " means fibre from the coat or fleece of alpaca, camel, goat, lamb, llama, rabbit, sheep, vicuna or yak, whether or not subjected to any process of manufacture or recovery.

22. What arrangements have been made regarding clothing for inmates of Institutions? A special issue of clothing coupons is to be made to institutions whose in-. mates have no food ration books. Institutions registered with the Ministry of Food for block food rationing, should therefore write immediately for Application Forms for coupons to the Assistant Secretary, Board of Trade (I. & M. 2), Pine Court, Bournemouth.

23. Must coupons be demanded against women's personal cutting-out service offers? Yes.

24. What about garments not shown on the lists published in this booklet? The number of coupons required for them will, in general, be that of the nearest like garment.

25. Are Local Authorities required to surrender coupons for their purchases? No. It is sufficient for them to certify a receipt for the goods, with which the shopkeeper will provide them.

26. Are coupons required for charitable gifts of clothing? It would be unfair if people were able to receive gifts bringing them above their ration. The charitable organisation must, therefore, collect coupons and surrender them to the Board of Trade if so directed. This also applies to bazaars and sales of work (see paragraph 47).

27. By buying a suit length and lining to hand back to the tailor for making-up may I not save a coupon or so? This may be the case in some instances, but, by and large, the coupons required for lengths and lining will not be less than the number required for a suit. See also paragraph 18.

28. What happens if clothing is lost by accident? If your stock of *essential* clothing is reduced below a certain minimum as a result of loss by fire or theft or in the laundry, or in any other accidental manner, then you should apply by post on a form (CRSC.1A) to a Collector of Customs and Excise whose address, together with the form of application, may be obtained from the nearest Information Centre of the Local Authority. Applicants are required to give on the form particulars of the essential articles of clothing and footwear they still possess, which will be taken into account in considering claims to extra coupons. Replacement coupons will not, however, be issued if the applicant still possesses sufficient articles of clothing to meet *essential* requirements.

The above procedure also applies in other exceptional cases, for example those discharged from a hospital or institution who find that their supply of clothing is below a certain minimum level.

29. Can people who have been bombed out get coupons? Yes, if their supply of essential clothing and footwear is brought below a certain level. They can obtain financial help, as well as coupons, by applying in person to the Assistance Board, or by post to a Collector of Customs and Excise, but in cases where coupons only are needed, the application should be made to a Collector of Customs and Excise (see paragraph 28). Applications to the Customs Authorities require to be accompanied by a completed form CRSC.1, obtainable from the Information Centre of any Local Authority.

30. When should coupons be detached if orders to the retailer are given by telephone? Before the goods are handed over the person delivering them must detach the correct number of coupons from the Food Book or Clothing Card.

31. Will shops sell without coupons to gain business? If they do, they and the customer seeking to evade the law in this manner will be acting contrary to the national interest and are also liable to heavy penalties (see paragraph 89). At the same time the stock of the shop will be run down, since new stocks need coupons.

32. What if my margarine coupons have been defaced by the grocer's rubber stamp? It doesn't matter. The retailer will accept them.

33. Are coupons required for presents of rationed goods sent to friends? Coupons must be surrendered when the rationed articles are first bought but coupons are not required when such articles are subsequently given away. You should on no account send loose coupons to your friends. This is an offence (see paragraph 74).

34. How do Local Authority Hospitals get their supplies? Local Authorities can purchase free of coupon (see paragraph 25).

35. Are there coupons for babies born after 1st June, 1941, and before Clothing Cards were issued? The new (4th Edition) Food Book must be taken to the Food Office where the baby's Clothing Card will be available. If the Clothing Card is issued before 1st December, 1941, it will contain 40 coupons; if issued during December, 1941, January or February, 1942 — 30 coupons; during March, April or May, 1942—20 coupons.

36. What about clothing and footwear for prisoners of war? Arrangements have been made between the Board of Trade and the War Organisation of the British Red Cross Society and the Order of St. John to enable next-of-kin to send clothing and footwear in their quarterly parcels to prisoners of war. A fund of 40 coupons will be issued in due course to next-of-kin for the purchase of such goods, and on receipt of the parcel at the packing centre at 14 Finsbury Circus, London, E.C.2, coupons will be returned to them to maintain their fund at the 40 level. The next-of-kin must include in their parcels the shop bills and a statement of the number of coupons used for each new article, which will be compared with the schedules issued by the Board of Trade. The number of coupons to be returned to senders of parcels will be decided by the War Organisation. The next-of-kin who have already sent parcels will have their coupons refunded and will also receive the 40 coupons from the War Organisation with their next quarterly label. *No special application should be made* in such cases. Those next-of-kin who are buying for the first time should either use their own coupons, or, if this is not possible, should apply to the above address for the necessary advance. Regimental Association secretaries and organisers of prisoners of war comforts funds approved by the War Organisation are requested to write to the above address for information concerning arrangements made for them.

37. Can " Butter and Margarine " coupons from the new (4th Edition) Food Book be used for clothing? No. Only those types of coupons illustrated in paragraph 8 are valid.

38. Are coupons required for a domestic servant's uniform? Yes. For cases where the employer provides it, see paragraph 42.

39. How can one send clothing to children evacuated overseas? Children in Canada, the United States of America, Newfoundland and certain other countries will still be able to receive parcels of clothing from their parents or guardians in this country. The Children's Overseas Reception Board, 45 Berkeley Street, London, W.1, will on request issue to the parents a special ration of 66 clothing coupons to allow them to carry on with their purchases.

40. How are plimsolls defined for rationing purposes? The definition of this is " a heelless shoe of any colour with canvas upper vulcanised to a rubber sole " and includes shoes of this description which are sold as tennis shoes.

41. Are goods required for Government contracts exempt? Yes.

Use the Subject Index on page ii

42. How are uniforms for bank messengers, waitresses and others engaged in civil occupations to be purchased ? Traders must collect the usual number of coupons per garment for uniforms supplied to an employer for his staff. A signed statement that the coupons were obtained by him for this purpose must be furnished by the employer. The rate of collection of the necessary coupons by the employer from the employees should be arranged between employer and staff.

43. Are coupons required for rationed goods supplied on hire or hire-purchase ? Rationed goods may be hired out for a period not exceeding 14 days without surrender of coupons. If, in any case, the goods are not returned the trader must furnish the Board of Trade by the 15th day of the following month with the particulars of the goods and the name and address of the person who has failed to return them. The customer will have contravened the Order if he fails to return the goods within 14 days ; and the supplier, when supplying the goods, must notify the customer of this provision.

Special arrangements are being made for theatrical costumiers.

In the case of hire-purchase, coupons must be surrendered *before* the goods are delivered.

44. What about laundry replacement service ? Coupons are needed for articles replaced.

For arrangements regarding *lost* articles, see paragraph 28.

45. If I get my old costume turned, do I need coupons ? Only if you have a new lining will you require coupons, according to the yardage used. If no new material is used, you will need no coupons.

46. Some schools require scholars to have big outfits. Are extra coupons available for these ? No special allowance is made. The schools and parents will have to get together and decide what is reasonable in the changed circumstances. By Autumn, when the school term starts, the child will have had his full 66 coupons, of which only 20 are to be reserved for use after 1st January, 1942. (See also paragraph 92.)

47. Do purchasers of goods at charity bazaars, sales of work and jumble sales have to give up coupons ? Since 5th August, 1941, it has not been permissible to sell any rationed article of clothing or footwear at bazaars or sales of work without the surrender of coupons. This also applies to secondhand articles. (See paragraph 65.) All coupons thus collected should be sent, together with a statement of the exact numbers and kinds of garments sold against them, to the Area Collection Centres of the Board of Trade.

Special arrangements are being made to permit the organisers of *bona fide* bazaars, etc., to secure rationed goods for sale at subsequent bazaars.

48. Do auctioned goods require coupons ? Yes, coupons must be collected by the auctioneer. (See also paragraph 49.)

49. If a retailer wishes to dispose of his business, what is the coupon position? The Board of Trade are prepared to licence the transfer of stocks of rationed goods from one retailer to another without coupons.

In cases where a retailer is giving up business and transferring it or the stocks to another retailer, the Board will also consider issuing a licence to enable him to transfer any coupons he may have on hand at the time of the sale.

50. How can district nurses obtain uniforms? Any nurse without uniform joining a District Nursing Association for duties which require indoor and/or outdoor uniform may, as an interim measure, purchase rationed goods (including piece goods) free of coupon against surrender to the trader of a certificate enumerating the requisite articles, and stating that the nurse requires them for her duties. This certificate must be signed by the Superintendent of the Association; it will then serve the trader in lieu of the equivalent number of coupons.

51. What is the position when goods are returned by the customer to the retailer as being unsuitable? The return of coupons is only permitted where the retailer agrees within 14 days of delivery to return the price of the articles originally chosen. As the returned coupons will then have been detached from the Food Book or Clothing Card, they may be used only in the same shop or for mail order purchases elsewhere.

52. Are there coupons for expectant mothers and newly-born babies? Yes, an extra allowance of 50 clothing coupons will be given to expectant mothers. These extra coupons are obtainable from the Public Health Department of the Local Authority for Maternity and Child Welfare. Certain areas of Northern Ireland have no child welfare centre, but application for the allowance may be made to the local authority.

The applicant has to get a certificate from the doctor or midwife booked to attend the confinement, or, if she attends an ante-natal clinic, from the Medical Officer of the clinic. This she should send by post or bring to the Public Health Department; if she has doubt about the address the doctor or midwife will tell her.

The certificate may be given as soon as pregnancy can safely be diagnosed and must state the name and address of the expectant mother, her National Registration identity card number, and the approximate date when her baby will be born. If twins are born, she can obtain an extra 50 coupons by applying again to the Public Health Department with their birth certificates; if they are diagnosed with certainty beforehand, she need not wait till they are born, as in this case a double issue will be made against the medical certificate of pregnancy.

Special clothing cards of 50 coupons will be issued later (about the end of August) as soon as printing and distribution can be completed, but, to avoid holding up the scheme till then, 10 Emergency Clothing Vouchers (blue), each equivalent to 5 coupons, will be issued to those who apply earlier. These are not quite so convenient to use as single coupons, and mothers who cannot make up the extra number of coupons with these vouchers when buying a batch of materials may prefer to use some of their own coupons and keep the blue vouchers for another time when they are buying rationed goods. If they do not want to start making their baby's clothes at once or can conveniently use coupons of their own for the time being, they will find it better to wait till the special cards are available.

The special ration will not be issued to mothers of babies born before the 5th August, 1941, as they will have bought maternity clothing and some at least of the materials for their baby's clothes before rationing started.

Besides the extra ration issued to the expectant mother, a ration will be issued for the baby after its birth (see paragraph 35).

53. Should I keep my old (Third Edition) Food Book? Most emphatically yes. The Clothing Card will be issued against this Food Book which you **must** keep when it has been replaced for food purposes by the new Food Book. Keep it after you have used up the 26 margarine coupons, until you change it for a Clothing Card.

54. Can I use my coupons for my children? Yes, the members of a family may pool their coupons.

55. What do I do about coupons sent to a supplier through the post, in a mail order transaction, **when he cannot supply the goods ordered?** Let him know whether you will leave the coupons on deposit to meet some future purchase from him, or whether you want them back for some other mail order business. Once the coupons are cut out they can only be used for mail order.

56. How do I get a Clothing Card after using all the margarine coupons in the Food Book? The margarine page ought, on the average, to last $4\frac{1}{2}$ months (26 coupons out of a year's ration of 66), but the new Clothing Card is now obtainable from the Post Office when it is required. Please don't apply for it until you need to. All the coupons from the Food Book should be used before you change it for a Clothing Card. If you have a few odd ones left and require to buy something that needs more than this number of coupons, order the article required and leave the odd coupons with your shopkeeper before you apply for the new Clothing Card.

57. What if I lose my Clothing Card? If satisfactory evidence of the loss is given, you will be able to obtain another (containing a reduced number of coupons) at one of the main Post Offices. False declaration will render the applicant liable to heavy penalties (see paragraph 89). You must, however, take every precaution not to lose your card, since you will not find it easy to get it replaced.

58. Do I have to give up coupons for mending wool? Mending wool cards or skeins of not more than $\frac{1}{4}$ ounce are coupon-free.

Use the Subject Index on page ii

59. Have any arrangements been made to provide clothing for theatrical productions? A committee has been set up to consider applications for coupons and to advise the Board of Trade. Such applications should be made to The Secretary, Theatrical Industry Rationing of Clothes Committee, Faraday House, 8/10 Charing Cross Road, London, W.C.2. This also applies to amateur productions.

60. Are coupons required for new or other gift clothing distributed by the W.V.S. to persons suffering from war distress? The W.V.S. can get supplies without coupons; but when they distribute clothing, it is only fair that they should collect coupons.

61. Where may I obtain further information on clothes rationing? From Citizen's Advice Bureaux, Women's Institutes and the W.V.S. Retailers can get help on trade questions from their local Chamber of Trade or Chamber of Commerce or from their Trade Association. These bodies are thus helping to keep the rationing scheme running as smoothly as possible.

62. Are coupons used in the Isle of Man valid here? In order to enable persons resident in the Isle of Man, which is not covered by the consumer rationing scheme in force in the United Kingdom, to purchase rationed goods on the mainland, and traders in the Isle of Man to obtain fresh stocks of rationed goods from mainland suppliers, clothing coupons issued by the Isle of Man Government under the Clothing Rationing Order, 1941, may be used in the United Kingdom, and accepted as equivalent to the coupons authorised for use in the United Kingdom under the Consumer Rationing Order made by the Board of Trade. Arrangements have been made by the Isle of Man Government for the coupons authorised for use in the United Kingdom under the Consumer Rationing Order to be used and accepted in the Isle of Man.

63. Can B.V.A.C. ambulance drivers obtain rationed clothing? Pending the conclusion of long-term arrangements, drivers of the British Volunteer Ambulance Corps may obtain supplies of rationed goods by signing a statement on a copy of the trader's bill that the articles mentioned represent their essential personal uniform requirements. This signed bill will serve the trader in lieu of the equivalent number of coupons.

64. Do coupons have to be given up when I have a garment renovated and the work entails the use of material which requires coupons? Yes. The number of coupons to be surrendered depends upon the amount of material used. But the trader is permitted to do the renovation without demanding coupons if $\frac{1}{4}$ coupon or less would have been required for the material. If the fraction works out at more than $\frac{1}{4}$ but less than 1, one coupon *must* be given up. For fractions in amounts above 1, see paragraph 99.

65. Do secondhand articles require coupons? If articles are genuine secondhand goods they do not need coupons if sold at or below prices fixed in accordance with the scale shown in par. 14. A pair of men's woollen socks, for example, which would require 3 coupons if new, can only be sold as secondhand without coupons if the selling price is not more than 8*d*. per coupon, *i.e.*, 2*s*. A pair of women's shoes which require 5 coupons if new can only be sold as secondhand without coupons if the price is not more than 1*s*. 6*d*. per coupon, *i.e.*, 7*s*. 6*d*.

66. What are the arrangements for voluntary hospitals ? Supplies of rationed goods to voluntary hospitals and other hospitals not covered by other arrangements may for the time being be made by traders without coupons against a letter of certificate to the effect that the goods, which must be specified as to quantity and type, have been supplied to the institution for its use.

67. Can men's cards be used to buy women's or children's goods and vice versa ? Yes, certainly, if the interchange is between members of the same family.

68. Can some of the coupons needed for an overcoat, for example, be cut from one person's card and some from another's ? Yes, if the people belong to the same family.

69. When do the coupons have to be handed over in the case of Clothing Clubs, and to whom ? The coupons have to be handed over to the supplier, before the goods are supplied. If the organiser of a Clothing Club wishes to obtain the goods by post, he must send the coupons before he can obtain delivery.

70. What is the procedure when the page of " Margarine " coupons has been cut out by the grocer and is still detached ? Where such a page has been recovered from the grocer with whom it has been deposited, the retailer may accept coupons from this detached page *only if the rest of the Food Book is produced at the same time.*

71. Can one buy a single shoe, sock, glove, or other article from a pair for half the number of coupons ? Yes, if the shopkeeper does not object.

72. Do coupons have to be given up for hats ? No. Headgear is coupon-free ; but scarves made up into headgear require coupons.

73. How can people who have been shipwrecked obtain clothing ? Passengers will be supplied with an initial outfit of clothing or coupons by the Public Assistance Authority or the Shipwrecked Mariners' Society acting on their behalf. The cases of officers and men in the Merchant Navy and that of fishermen are dealt with in paragraph 80.

74. Am I allowed to give loose coupons to the shopkeeper in exchange for rationed goods ? To offer or accept loose coupons is an offence (see paragraph 89). The only exceptions to this rule are certain special cases such as when an employer is buying uniforms for his staff (see paragraph 42), or in the case of orders by post (when the coupons should be signed on the back).

It is not permissible to give coupons by way of change. If a customer has been given strip-tickets in units of 5 or 10 coupons, by, for example, the Assistance Board, and wishes to buy a garment requiring say 7 coupons, he should make up the two coupons out of his ordinary ration card.

75. How can knitting wool in Service colours be obtained for making comforts for the Forces ? The knitter must apply for registration to her local branch of the British Legion, British Legion (Women's Section), the Women's Co-operative Guild, the National Federation of Women's Institutes, or the Women's Voluntary Services for Civil Defence, or to such other nation-wide organisations as may be announced later. No person may be registered with more than one such organisation for the purpose, and on registration her Clothing Card (or old Food Book) will be endorsed with the name of the organisation with whom she is registered. The applicant must provide satisfactory evidence that she has a relation or friend in the Forces, serving away from his or her home, and must give the regimental number or unit. No one may receive more than 1½ lb. of wool in the year ending 31st August, 1942, for knitting comforts ; any more wool required will have to be obtained with the knitter's own coupons.

Working parties whose members are not individually registered with any of the above-mentioned organisations will only be able to obtain coupon-free supplies of knitting wool for comforts for the Forces if affiliated to one of the Service organisations, namely :— *Navy*—(1) Depôt for Knitted Garments for the Royal Navy ; (2) Navy League Seafarers' Comforts Supply : *Army*—Director of Voluntary Organisations : *Air Force*—Royal Air Force Comforts Committee.

76. What has to be done with the clothing coupons of someone who has died ? They should be returned to the local Registrar of Births and Deaths with the Food Book.

77. How can discharged members of H.M. Forces (including the Nursing Services) obtain civilian clothing ? They should, for the time being, apply to a Local Information Centre for Form CRSC.1A, and follow the procedure outlined in paragraph 28.

78. How can members of the Allied Red Cross obtain uniform clothing ? Pending the conclusion of long-term arrangements, uniformed personnel of recognised Allied Red Cross Committees may now purchase coupon-free uniform clothing on (a) presenting to the shop a Red Cross membership card, (b) signing a statement on the back of the trader's bill that the goods represent essential personal requirements of uniform, and (c) giving after the signature the address of the Red Cross Committee concerned and the unit number (if any) of the member.

The Allied Red Cross Committees recognised by the British

Red Cross are the Belgian, Czechoslovak, Netherland, Norwegian and Polish Red Cross Committees in London. The bill as signed above will serve the retailer in lieu of coupons.

79. Must I give coupons when I buy cloth for household furnishing ? This is rationed, but certain furnishing fabrics may be sold without coupons to members of the public. These can be bought from the retailer either by the yard, or made-up, or made-to-measure (see paragraph 13). For sheets, towels, dusters, etc., see paragraph 88.

80. How do men in the Merchant Navy and fishermen obtain their clothing ? Arrangements have been made for the supply without coupons, of clothing to officers and men of the Merchant Navy and fishermen who are in need of this clothing for service at sea or who have been shipwrecked. Particulars of these arrangements can be obtained at Mercantile Marine offices, but retailers should note that for the present they may sell clothes and footwear without the surrender of coupons against certificates issued by superintendents of Mercantile Marine offices. Shipwrecked mariners may apply alternatively to the Shipwrecked Mariners' Society.

81. What is the position regarding the supply of rationed uniform clothing to Members of the British Red Cross Society, St. John Ambulance Brigade and Members of the War Organisation of the British Red Cross Society and Order of St. John, including trained nurses, **also the Members of the Women's Transport Service (F.A.N.Y.) ?** Members of these Organisations may obtain their essential personal requirements of rationed uniform clothing and footwear without coupons during the period until final arrangements have been made to provide them with supplies of clothing coupons.

Officers and Members of the British Red Cross Society, of the St. John Ambulance Brigade and Officers of the War Organisation of the B.R.C.S. and Order of St. John may obtain supplies of rationed goods by signing a statement on the back of the trader's bill that the articles mentioned represent their essential personal uniform requirements. Trained nurses of the War Organisation B.R.C.S. and Order of St. John may obtain similar facilities. The rank of the Officer or Member and the County and number of Detachment should be shown in the case of the B.R.C.S. and in the case of the St. John Ambulance Brigade the rank of the Officer or Member and the County and name of the Division must be given. Trained Nurses of the War Organisation must intimate their membership of that body.

Non-commissioned Officers and men of the War Organisation will continue to obtain supplies of uniform from the Uniform Department of the War Organisation.

The Officers of the Women's Transport Service (F.A.N.Y.) Corps Units may obtain supplies of rationed goods by signing a statement on the back of the trader's bill that the articles mentioned represent their essential personal uniform requirements. The rank and unit should be indicated. Non-commissioned Officers and other ranks may obtain similar facilities provided that a document is attached to the bill signed by the Officer-in-Charge, Women's Transport Service (F.A.N.Y.) Headquarters, testifying that the goods represent essential personal uniform requirements.

82. What about civilian personnel employed with H.M. Forces? Until military clothing coupons are issued, retailers are authorised to supply civilian personnel paid by and attached to Army establishments or units, and who are supplied with rationed foodstuffs by the Army authorities and thus have no civilian ration cards, with their essential personal requirements of clothing, provided these are detailed on a document signed by the Commanding Officer of the unit concerned and bearing its office stamp. The document will be surrendered to the retailer at the time of purchase.

83. What arrangements are there for manual workers who, because of the nature of their employment, wear out their clothing and footwear more quickly than other people, and of those who require protective clothing? Industrial concerns, including mines and quarries, can now purchase for their employees types of overalls which are not exempt from the Consumer Rationing Order and other protective clothing and footwear, necessary for safety or health, without coupons. Concerns wanting to avail themselves of

this arrangement must obtain a certificate from one of H.M. Inspectors of Factories or Mines stating that the clothing, the nature and quantities of which must be specified, is required for safety or health. This certificate is from the trader's point of view equivalent to the number of coupons for the clothing.

Other cases mentioned in the question are still under consideration by the Board in consultation with the industries concerned.

84. May a person entering H.M. Forces give his coupons to members of his family or to any other person? No. He has to surrender them to the responsible Naval, Military or Air Force Authorities.

85. Are coupons required for orders given before 1st June, 1941? These require coupons, even if a deposit has been paid.

86. Is it permissible for relatives of a family to pool their coupons with those of the family so as to give a bride a trousseau? Yes, but remember that the Ration Books or Clothing Cards must be taken to the shop whenever purchases are made and coupons must only be cut out by the retailer.

87. Won't I run short of clothes next winter? Not if you PLAN the use of your coupons. You will have 66 coupons for the year in all, 26 of them in your January-June, 1941, Food Book, 40 when you get your Clothing Card. Think over your general needs for the year and decide how you may best spread the ration. You should allow for winter needs and leave coupons over for casual purchases.

88. Are such things as sheets, serviettes and table - cloths rationed ? Ready-made household textile articles are not rationed, but if you buy stuff in the piece to make up yourself, or have it made up to your own requirements, it is rationed and needs coupons (see also paragraph 79).

89. May I sell coupons I don't need, or may I buy other people's spare coupons ? No, it is illegal and subject to heavy penalties. (On summary conviction for a contravention of the Consumer Rationing Orders, a person may be imprisoned for 3 months or fined up to £100, or both. On conviction on indictment the penalty is up to two years' imprisonment or a fine not exceeding £500, or both.)

90. What is the position regarding cut rug wool ? All knitting wool is rationed ; if wool, therefore, can be used for knitting, coupons are required for it ; if, however, it is cut into small pieces, and it is impossible to use it for knitting purposes, it can be sold free of coupons.

91. Collar attached to shirt—how many coupons are needed for this ? Collars sold separately require coupons, but a shirt with collar attached counts as a shirt and requires 7 coupons if woollen and 5 if made of other material for adults' sizes, and 6 and 4 respectively for children's sizes.

92. What provision has been made for the fact that growing children require a good many clothes ? The number of coupons for articles of children's clothing and footwear is lower than that for adults. For those children who are too big to wear children's sizes, extra coupons will be issued and the details will be published later.

93. Children under four are often as big as those of six or seven. Are coupons needed for their ready-made clothes according to the children's or to the infants' scale ? The test is size and not age in these cases.

94. If I buy goods with " thrift tickets " or other tokens in lieu of cash, are coupons required ? Yes, because in fact coupons are required whenever rationed goods are *supplied*.

95. Are furs rationed ? Fur skins are unrationed, but fur ties require 5 coupons (5 coupons *per skin* in the case of fox-fur ties) and fur coats are rated as coats, according to their size. All other garments of fur or imitation fur are rationed.

96. What if I make my own clothes ? If you are of average size and choose economical patterns you should gain slightly by making your own clothes, especially skirts and blouses. You can save considerably by making clothes for children aged four to seven.

97. Is there any allowance for socks and shirts for officers and other ranks of the Home Guard and A.T.C. ? There is no special allowance as they already have the full ration of coupons for their current requirements.

98. When goods are sent out on approval, must coupons be surrendered? Rationed goods may be supplied on approval without coupons for a period not exceeding 14 days provided the customer first states the quantity and description of the goods he desires to purchase, and surrenders the appropriate number of coupons. A woman ordering a woollen skirt, for instance, must send 6 coupons. The trader can then send a selection of skirts from which the customer can make her choice. If she does not return the unselected skirts within 14 days, the trader must send particulars to the Board of Trade by the fifteenth day of the following month.

If more goods are kept than were originally intended, the appropriate number of coupons must be sent.

99. What happens when the number of coupons to be given up includes a fraction? Coupons must in no circumstances be cut into pieces. The fraction should be made up to the nearest whole number if it is half or more. If it is less than a half, it should be ignored, except that where the number comes to less than 1, it counts as 1; e.g., $5\frac{1}{2}$ or $5\frac{2}{3}$ counts as 6, $5\frac{1}{8}$ counts as 5, but $\frac{1}{8}$ counts as 1. For the purpose of finding exactly how many coupons should be given up, all purchases made at the same time should be added together, e.g., a yard of 54-in. wool cloth sold at the same time as a large handkerchief make $4\frac{1}{2}$ plus $\frac{1}{2}$, which equals 5 coupons.

100. Does a gift of clothing to a charitable institution require coupons? If you buy rationed goods to give to a charitable institution you must surrender coupons for their purchase, but no coupons have to be handed over by the institution authorities when they receive these gifts.

101. Further Information

This booklet is a guide to the working of the Consumer Rationing Orders, 1941.* Its contents do not in any way alter the provisions of the Orders. Enquiries by the public should be made in the first instance to one of the authorities mentioned in the preceding pages. Traders should consult the Secretary of their Chamber of Trade, Chamber of Commerce or other trade organisation. Enquiries which cannot be dealt with by these organisations should be addressed thus:

Enquirer	Department concerned
Members of the public and retailers.	Board of Trade, Pine Court, Bournemouth.
Unregistered makers-up ...	Board of Trade, Marsham Court, Bournemouth.
Persons registered under the Limitation of Supplies Order.	Board of Trade, Carlton Hotel, Bournemouth.

* S. R. & O. 1941, Nos. 701, 939, price 3d. each, S. R. & O. 1941, No. 1011, price 1d., S. R. & O. 1941, Nos. 1012-1018, price 2d., inclusive, S. R. & O. 1941, No. 1176, price 2d., and S. R. & O. 1941, Nos. 1189 and 1195, price 1d. each, published by His Majesty's Stationery Office. Postage 1d. extra in each case.

*   *   *

To be purchased directly from H.M. STATIONERY OFFICE at the following addresses: York House, Kingsway, London, W.C.2; 120 George Street, Edinburgh, 2; 39-41 King Street, Manchester, 2; 1 St. Andrew's Crescent, Cardiff; 80 Chichester Street, Belfast; or through any bookseller.

Sept., 1941. (2978) Ps. 3108 Wt. 1986 40M. 9/41 W.P. Ltd.

51—9999.

Deft Darns

by Mrs. SEW-&-SEW

DO'S AND DONT'S

DO darn on the wrong side directly a thin place appears.

— tack a piece of net on a large hole and darn across it for extra strength (see linen darn).

— darn well beyond the weak place.

— leave loops at the turns to allow for shrinking.

— settle yourself comfortably in a good light before you start.

DON'T wait for a hole to develop.

— make straight edges to your darns; a little irregularity distributes the strain.

— pull the thread taut or it will pucker.

— expect to make a success of a job by hit-or-miss methods.

Neat darns, done in good time, can make things last without making them look shabby. Here are some hints on every day darns and how to set about them. Some general rules, too, for repairs that pay.

ISSUED BY THE BOARD OF TRADE

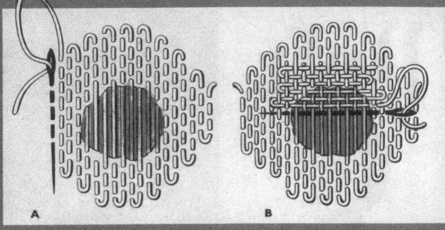

TO DARN A HOLE

A First clear the loops of fluff and broken ends of threads from knitted garments or clip away ragged edges from machine knit fabrics. Always use a darning ball under large holes.

1 Make the darn the shape of the hole.
2 Darn up and down the hole first; work on the wrong side.
3 Choose mending as fine as the material of the garment.
4 Begin a good distance away from the hole in order to reinforce the thin parts round the hole.
5 Space the rows of darning the width of a strand of mending apart.
6 Pick up the backs of the loops only unless the material is very fine.
7 Leave loops at the ends of each row and darn so that stitches alternate with spaces between stitches in the previous rows.

8 Pick up the edge of the hole in one row then go over the edge of the hole in the next row. If you have cleared the edges of the hole you will find this will be easy and will make a neater mend on the right side of the garment.
9 Continue the darn over the thin place beyond the hole.

B Darning over the first rows of Darning

1 Darn over the hole only and about two stitches of darning beyond.
2 Leave loops at the ends of each row and only pick up on the needle the darning stitches.
3 Pick up the alternate strands of mending in first row.
4 In alternate rows, pick up the strands of mending you passed over in the previous row.

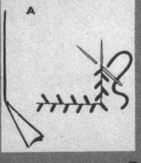

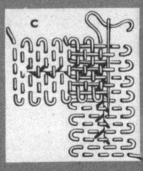

DARNING A TEAR

A Before darning a tear, tack down on a piece of paper and fish-bone stitch the edges of tear together.

B Darn well beyond tear right across base, forming a rectangle.

C Turn the work round and darn in the same way across the other part of tear. At the corner a solid square is formed. Remove tacking thread and paper.

TO DARN A KNITTED FABRIC

The first stage in darning
on knitted fabrics is the
same as an ordinary darn,
but the direction of the
second set of stitches is
diagonal.

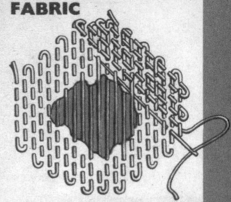

TO REPAIR TORN BUTTONHOLES

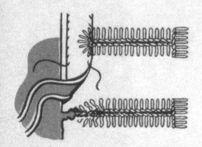

Usually it is the outer edges of
buttonholes that " go ". To tidy
and strengthen them, stitch a
length of tape or a narrow band
of matching material along the
edge of the garment. Then re-do
the buttonholing over the new
material (*Diagram*).

TO DARN A STOCKING LADDER

Work on the right side and use a fine,
steel crochet hook. Place it into a
dropped loop and draw the straight
thread above it through the loop. Repeat as necessary. Have a needle ready
threaded, darn in from above ladder and
towards it. Pass needle through the
crocheted loop and darn back to start.
Bring up any further runs in the ladder
and finish off in the same way.

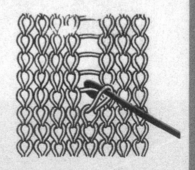

TO JOIN LOCKNIT SEAMS

(1) Buttonhole stitch each side of slit.

(2) Draw knots of buttonhole stitches together with oversewing stitches. This material is suitable, too, for mending straight tears in gloves, leather jackets or furs as it lessens the strain on the material.

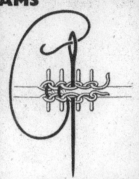

TO DARN A SLIT

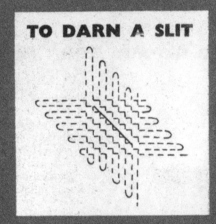

(1) Darn in rows across cut. The edge of row of darning should be parallel with cut. (2) Darn across the cut in the opposite direction—the edge of the darn again parallel with the cut.

TO DARN LINEN

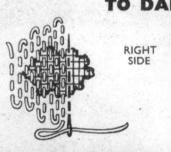

RIGHT SIDE

WRONG SIDE

A particularly neat and easy darn can be made on pillow-cases, tablecloths and table napkins, by lightly tacking a scrap of net over the hole on the wrong side, and darning in and out of it on the right side. Trim away the surplus edges on the wrong side after darning. Where invisible mending is not essential, this type of darn can be used for any kind of material not subject to frequent laundering.

A.4880 Wt. 24565 200,000 8 45 Gp 961 Fosh & Cross Ltd., London.   B.O.T. 18L

save fuel

ALL ALONG THE LINE

Directly or indirectly, Fuel enters almost daily into the domestic business of washing, drying, ironing and so forth, and since fuel must be saved "all along the line" this pamphlet has been prepared to help housewives to save fuel whilst actually improving the results of their work.

HOT WATER—AND THE FUEL NEEDED TO MAKE IT HOT

Do you know, it takes about one quarter of all the fuel used in the average home to make cold water hot. Yet you'll find it quite easy to economise on hot water if you study the following practical hints, and you'll certainly make a substantial saving of fuel.

For example :—

HOT WATER ON WASH DAY

Apart from baby things which make frequent small washings unavoidable, one wash day a week instead of three or four means not only a big saving in fuel but a valuable saving also of time, labour and expense. Each wash, no matter how small, calls for certain preparations and of course, a good deal of " clearing up " afterwards. So in every way

SMALL WASHES ARE WASTEFUL

Another important consideration is the temperature of the water and the quantity used. The hotter the water, the more fuel is needed. Using water no warmer than is absolutely necessary means using less fuel. " Plenty of hot water " may have been all right when fuel was plentiful. To-day, with winter fuel more and more precious, the commonsense rule must be "as little hot water as possible", and even that no hotter than necessary.

Washing & Ironing

Thousands of women are to-day washing and ironing things at home which in peace-time they sent to the laundry. Many war-time materials they wash and iron call for more-than-ordinary care and treatment. Since clothes are so precious and hard to come by nowadays, the following " ways and means " will well repay your making fullest use of them. For easy reference, they are divided into two sections.

ALWAYS....

ALWAYS spread rayon out to dry in the shade so that the weight of the garment is evenly distributed. For instance, dresses should be hung over the line at the waist.

ALWAYS test the iron on a pad of paper before ironing. If any scorch mark appears in 15-20 seconds, iron is too hot.

ALWAYS save the ironing of towels, sheets and other household linens by partially folding before quite dry and putting through wringer.

ALWAYS iron shantung and tussore garments bone dry. Stockings are best left unironed. The natural heat of the leg will eliminate any small creases there may be in the stockings, whatever the material from which they may be woven.

ALWAYS when washing gloves put them on your hands. This helps them to keep their shape. Lined gloves should be dry cleaned.

ALWAYS rinse cotton and linen clothes thoroughly and dry in the shade. You need only iron them while slightly damp with a fairly hot iron.

ALWAYS run your dusters and household cloths through any soapy water left over from your other washing.

NEVER....

NEVER use very hot water for rayons. Dirt stays on the surface, so hard rubbing is quite unnecessary. And of course, never peg rayons. Pegging may permanently mark the material.

NEVER sprinkle rayons. It leaves them looking patchy. If the material is too dry, re-wet it and dry again.

NEVER leave any articles bunched together when wet, especially rayons which may crease, and coloured things which may run.

NEVER leave damp clothes wrapped up for days before ironing them. Iron as soon as possible after washing.

NEVER wash suede gloves and never put leather gloves near fire or radiator. Try rinsing leather gloves in plain warm water first ; this often gets them clean. If not, wash them in warm soapy water.

NEVER dry coloured materials in strong sunlight : it bleaches them. Never wash coloured articles along with white ones.

ALWAYS....

ALWAYS soak over-night all white linens, cottons and articles which you are quite sure will not shrink or run.

ALWAYS rinse woollens thoroughly, lifting the whole of the garment out of the water at once, squeezing gently all the time (not wringing) so that the weight of the water does not stretch it.

NEVER....

NEVER boil or soak woollens, or lift them out of the water while you are washing them.

NEVER rub, twist or wring woollen articles when washing them. Rubbing shrinks and felts wool. Never hang woollen textures when wet, otherwise they may stretch.

SOME SOAP-SAVING TIPS

(1) Use soft water or rain water wherever possible
(2) Save all scraps of soap and dissolve them together in an equal quantity of boiling water. Add when cold to washing water.

(3) If you haven't soap-flakes handy, shred soap finely into boiling water. Then add enough cold water for your purpose.

... MAKING THE MOST OF WHAT YOU HAVE

Since we must save all the fuel we can, we must, of course, make the most of what we have. Wise planning of fuel consumption will make saving easier all round. These hints will show the way. First of all—

HAVE YOU AN OPEN FIRE WITH A BACK BOILER ?

The proper use of fire-bricks with open fires will make a wonderful difference to your coal bill. If you are not sure how to fix these, your ironmonger or builders' merchant will soon explain. A fire-brick can be fitted at each side of the grate, but not, of course, at the back where it would cover the boiler and the boiler flue inlet. There are also " pyramid " shaped bricks for the middle of the fire.

IS YOUR GRATE FITTED WITH A FRET ?

This " fret " controls the air supply passing up through the fire. Never roar the fire : aim at a smallish fire with a steady rate of burning. When the boiler is being used, the fire should be built up well over the flue opening at the back of the grate

and covered with a layer of slack to prevent cold air from being drawn into the flue and chilling the boiler.

IS YOURS A COMBINATION GRATE ?

A combination grate has an open fire, a hot water boiler and an oven. When you want to cook or to heat water, build up the fire over the oven or boiler flue inlet and cover it with a layer of slack to keep out the cold air. Open the appropriate damper and shut the others.

FIRE-BRICKS AND COMBINATION GRATES

In most combination grates, a fire-brick can be fitted at the side of the grate opposite to the oven flue. Be careful not to cover the flue inlets, either to the oven or the boiler.

Geysers & Heaters

Gas Geysers, Gas and Electric Water Heaters, Coppers and Domestic Boilers are capable of consuming a tremendous amount of fuel unless carefully supervised. The hints below will help you.

GAS GEYSERS AND GAS HEATERS

Never use the geyser or the gas storage heater for small quantities of water. You'll save gas by heating small quantities in a kettle. It is a good plan when heating large quantities of water, e.g., for laundering, to arrange for other hot water jobs to be done at the same time.

ELECTRIC WATER HEATERS

As far as possible, keep heater switched off during the day-time (especially between 8 a.m. and 1 p.m.) and do the water heating at night. As with gas heaters, try to arrange as many hot water jobs as possible at the same time as laundering.

DOMESTIC BOILERS

Can you arrange hot water needs so that the boiler is not used more than two days a week? But if a fair quantity of hot water is needed within, say, 30 hours, it's more economical to bank the boiler than to let the fire go out and have to re-light it. The fire should burn at a slow steady rate. Never allow it to roar.

HAVE YOU A COPPER?

The three main points to watch :—

(1) Never put more water in the copper than you really need,

(2) Keep a clean fire and aim at a steady rate of burning, and

(3) Do not let the fire roar.

HEATING WASH WATER IN TUBS

If you have to heat your wash water in tubs on the kitchen range or a gas stove, the first thing to remember is not to put in more water than you actually need. This is most important when using a gas stove. Try using water not quite as hot as usual. This saves time and fuel.

A FEW WORDS ABOUT "LAGGING"

Where you have a hot water tank and piping you can save a great deal of fuel by making sure that the tank and pipes are lagged. "Lagging" means wrapping up the tank and pipes so that the heat is kept *inside*. For fuller instructions about this most important way of saving fuel send a post-card to :

PUBLICITY DIVISION,
MINISTRY of FUEL & POWER
7 Millbank, London, S.W.1.

ISSUED BY THE MINISTRY OF FUEL AND POWER

Printed for H.M. Stationery Office by Fosh & Cross Ltd. 51-1037.

THE A·B·C OF MAKING
BUTTONHOLES

Different Types and where to use them.

WORKED BUTTONHOLES (Section I overleaf) are best for linens, cottons and silks.

TAILORS' BUTTONHOLES (Section II overleaf) are suitable for heavier materials and for men's clothes.

BOUND BUTTONHOLES (Section III overleaf) are recommended for really large buttons or where the material frays easily.

N.B. Make horizontal buttonholes for coats, jackets, and all fitted garments. For looser things like shirts and blouses, the buttonholes should be vertical.

by Mrs. SEW & SEW

NEAT, firm buttonholes are important; they last longer and look better. If you follow these directions closely, you will avoid the untidy home-made air which comes from puckered or frayed buttonholes. Remember that for women's clothes, buttonholes go on the right, while for men they are worked on the left.

● GUIDE TO SPACING

Cut a length of cardboard and nick it at evenly spaced intervals. Lay this parallel with the front edge of the garment, about half-an-inch in from the extreme edge. Run tacking thread to mark this line. Put in pins where each buttonhole is to be made (**A**) Measure from tacking line to $\frac{1}{4}''$ wider than button and place pin at end to prevent cutting too far (**B**).

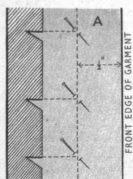

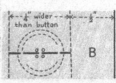

WORKED BUTTONHOLES

(Diagrams for women's wear)

SECTION I

Tack each side of buttonhole line (**a**). Cut the slit straight by the thread of the material and overcast (**b**). Work from left to right, using buttonhole stitch. At the end of buttonhole, overcast, pulling the sewing thread lightly to form half an eyelet (**c**). Continue along other side of buttonhole, using buttonhole stitch. Make a bar at far end of buttonhole by taking two or three strands across and then buttonhole-stitching over these strands. Take the needle into the material as well as over the strands (**d**).

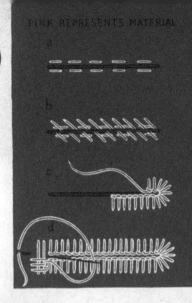

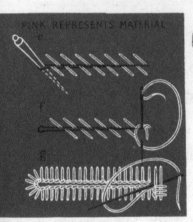

TAILORS' BUTTONHOLES

(Diagrams for men's wear)

SECTION II

Punch a hole at front of slit, overcast edges of slit (**e**). Thread your needle without a knot and run it into the material an inch from the far end of slit. Bring needle out at the end of slit (**f**). Work from right to left. Work all round the punched hole with buttonhole stitch. Make two or three strands across bar end of buttonhole and then buttonhole-stitch the strands together. Do not take the needle into the material (**g**).

BOUND BUTTONHOLES

(Diagrams for women's wear)

SECTION III

Mark the position of the buttonhole on the right side with stitches which can be seen on the wrong side too. Cut a strip of material 1½ ins. longer than the buttonhole and about 2½ ins. wide. Tack to right side of garment with right sides facing. Machine-stitch through both thicknesses all round space for buttonhole as shown (**h**) leaving from ⅛ in. to ½ in. between rows of stitching. Cut down the middle, snip corners and pull material through to wrong side (**i**). Press well. On the wrong side, turn under edges of the bind to make hems just wide enough to hem down over the stitching (**j**). Make little pleats at the ends of the buttonholes so that the binding will be flat.

F4410 Wt.55187 120,000 3/45 Gp.961 Fosh & Cross Ltd.
B. O. T. 16L

Getting ready for baby

—it's surprising how little you really need buy

IF you are going to have a baby here are some of the many things you will want to know about baby clothes, prams, cots, maternity clothes and, of course, the important question of extra coupons.

First of all, try to borrow as much of your equipment as possible from a friend—clothes, pram, etc. But if you are unlucky and have to make the clothes from old material or new the Welfare Centre or Health Visitor will advise you.

BABY'S COUPONS AND YOURS

For information about extra coupons ask your Medical Officer of Health or Health Visitor.

PLAN YOUR COUPONS CAREFULLY from the very beginning and you will find them sufficient for your needs.

Babies don't need nearly as many clothes as people used to think—they must be clothed lightly and sufficiently cosily to keep the skin warm to the touch.

A layette which is a mixture of knitted and material garments is the most suitable, because the wind blows through an outfit that has not one thickness of material among the knitted garments. Pure wool or a mixture of wool and artificial silk can be used for vests.

HERE IS A SUGGESTED LAYETTE

4–5 gowns (material) to be used by day and night, 22″–24″ long, taking up to 1½ yards 36″ material each.

4 vests (woven or knitted).

3 matinée jackets (2 oz. wool each).

3 pairs bootees (2 oz. wool).

2 medium-sized shawls (about 8 oz. of wool each).

Turkish towelling napkins.

Muslin napkins—never buy more napkins than you really need, remember fair shares !

INESSENTIALS

Rubber knickers—are not necessary and, quite apart from the fact that rubber is very scarce, they are very uncomfortable for the baby.

Head shawls and gloves—the baby should be quite warm enough if wrapped cosily in shawl or blanket.

Pilches—are not needed ; napkins, put on properly, can look very neat, and the extra layer is inclined to overheat.

HINTS ON MAKING BABY'S LAYETTE

DON'T go in for frills and trimmings and elaborate designs when making Baby's layette. You must aim to make the clothes from as little material as possible, yet in such a way that they are loose and Baby can wear them longer than he would have worn his first clothes in peace-time.

Simple magyar shapes free from constricting bands are best for gowns and jackets made of material, as tucks can be put on the shoulders, the neck can be made larger as Baby grows, and there is no restriction under the arms. Tucks near the hem and in the sleeves are a great economy in the long run. Baby's first gowns can later be adapted as petticoats and nightgowns and dresses for quite a long time.

Small tabs of tape sewn to the front lower edge of the vest will provide a firm hold for safety-pins and prevent tearing.

HERE ARE TWO OF THE BEST DESIGNS

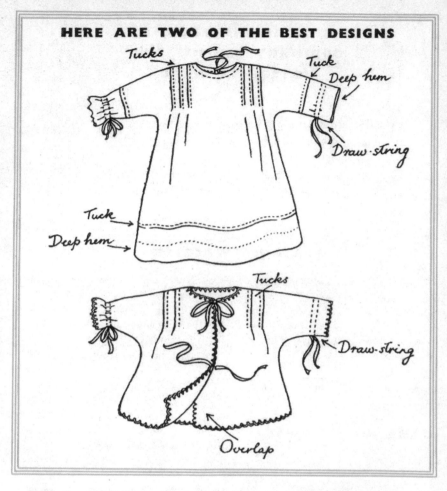

Tucks
Tuck
Deep hem
Draw-string
Tuck
Deep hem
Tucks
Draw-string
Overlap

The local Welfare Centre or your Health Visitor will be ready to advise you

COTS.—A laundry basket, or even a deep drawer suitably lined and padded, can be adapted to make a very useful cot for the first months. No permit is required for a Utility cot.

BEDCLOTHES.—If you live in the country there is probably no need to buy a mattress. A corn chandler or farmer may be able to sell you some clean chaff. Bake it in a moderate oven for one hour, then fill a pillow-case with it. A small piece of old blanket or rug should be placed under chaff mattresses to provide warmth in winter.

If a pillow is thought necessary a small flat pillow-case can also be filled with chaff.

ADAPTING YOUR ORDINARY CLOTHES FOR MATERNITY WEAR

Try to avoid spending coupons on special maternity clothes. Almost all your existing clothes can be altered easily so that you can wear them comfortably until the baby is born, and you can wear them again afterwards. For instance, why not put in an attractive matching or contrasting gathered or pleated panel in the front of the dress?

WASHING WOOLLENS

To wash the baby's woollens, make a lather with warm—*not hot*—water. Make quite sure that all the soap is dissolved, then gently squeeze the woollens through and rinse them in clear water of the same heat as the first lot.

Never Boil—Never Soak—Never Rub.

To dry woollens lay them flat and pull them into the right shape and size on something like a small string hammock, in the open air, so that the air will be able to circulate.

WASHING NAPKINS.—Soak first and then wash in hot soapy water. Finish off by boiling.

CARE OF PRAMS:

Try to do small repairs yourself, and do them in time. Most dealers will do major repairs.

Use your soapy water on washing day to give the pram a good wash.

Dry it thoroughly afterwards and see that no soap is left on the tyres.

If you should be caught in a shower wipe the pram dry as soon as possible, making sure that any mud is removed and that the wheels and tyres as well as metal parts are quite dry.

Avoid wheeling the pram over gravel. Only substitute rubber can be used for new tyres these days and this needs more care than rubber.

Use the hood as little as possible because, although Baby's eyes should be protected from the bright sunlight, he does need daylight and air.

A few drops of oil to wheel joints will keep the pram running smoothly.

HOW TO PATCH SHEETS AND BLANKETS

by

Mrs. Sew - and - Sew

★ When choosing piece for patch, make sure the selvedge runs the same way as on the article to be patched. Patches on household linen should be edge-stitched by machine and the corners made square and very strong. If the area to be patched is very near the edge, make the patch large enough to reach the edge allowing sufficient material to make hem along the outer side, or round new corner.

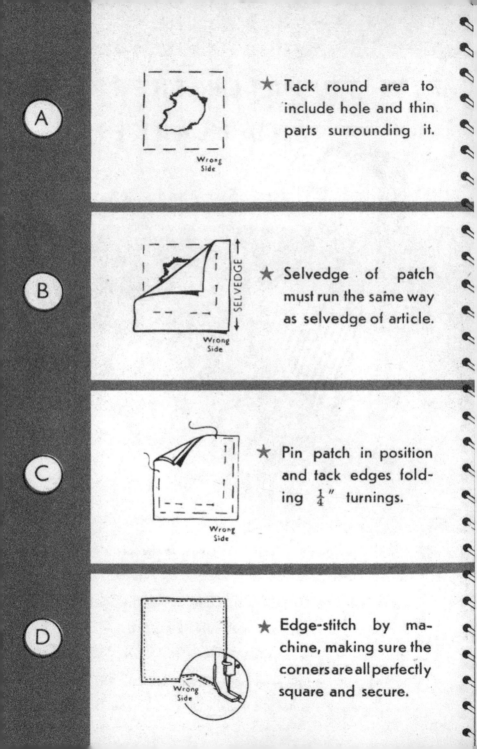

A

★ Tack round area to include hole and thin parts surrounding it.

Wrong Side

B

★ Selvedge of patch must run the same way as selvedge of article.

SELVEDGE

Wrong Side

C

★ Pin patch in position and tack edges folding ¼″ turnings.

Wrong Side

D

★ Edge-stitch by machine, making sure the corners are all perfectly square and secure.

Wrong Side

E

Right
Side

★ Turn to the right side and cut towards the four corners leaving slightly less than $\frac{1}{2}''$ for a good $\frac{1}{4}''$ hem with ample turning.

F

Right
Side

★ Then fold back the four worn sections from corner cut to corner cut. Cut off.

G

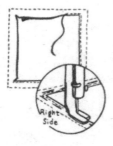

Right
Side

★ Make a diagonal snip at each corner slightly less than $\frac{1}{4}''$, the width of the first turning. Turn in and machine stitch.

H

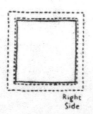

Right
Side

★ Completed patch on right side.

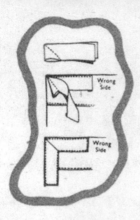

★ Three stages of strengthening the corner of sheet with tape by machine.

1. Take a length of tape—about 8 inches. Fold in half and stitch as shown.

2. Pin or tack this to wrong side of sheet, with the mitred or stitched part at the sheet corner.

3. Machine stitch all round.

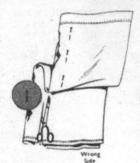

★ If sheet is worn in the middle, fold and cut away the thin part.

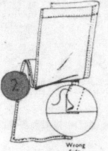

Hem the cut edges by machine and overlap selvedges and stitch (as inset)

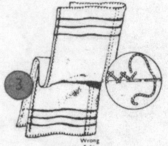

Blankets may be cut in the same way and selvedges joined by loose seaming.

★ A patch on a blanket is similar to a cotton patch but with edges left raw and herring-boned.

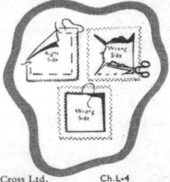

F3865 Wt. 42713 120,120 12/44 Gp961 Fosh & Cross Ltd.   Ch.L-4

ISSUED BY THE BOARD OF TRADE

HOW TO REINFORCE FOR EXTRA WEAR

by Mrs. SEW-and-SEW

Re-inforcing is strengthening a new garment at places where you know the wear will be greatest. It is always done on the wrong side and it should not show on the right side if it is neatly sewn. Use hemming for most work, but herringbone stitch should be used on woven fabrics and flannel, when the edges are left raw. Tape or bias binding will be found useful for strengthening seams.

FOR RE-INFORCING ELBOWS, KNEES, ETC.

Sew an extra piece of cloth inside. Keep it in position by hemming opposite sides. It should be slightly tighter than the section it protects.

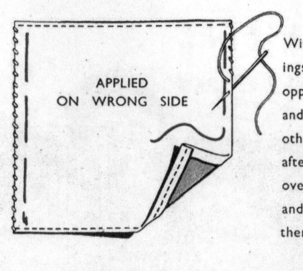

APPLIED ON WRONG SIDE

With $\frac{1}{4}$ in. turnings hem the opposite sides and leave the other sides free after turning over the edges and neatening them as shown.

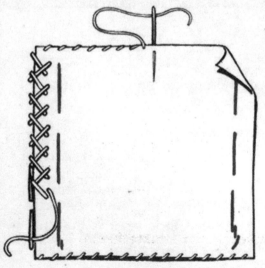

Showing method for herring-bone stitch for use on woven fabrics and flannel. Oversew the free edges.

LININGS

Linings can easily be strengthened, as they can be partly removed while being sewn.

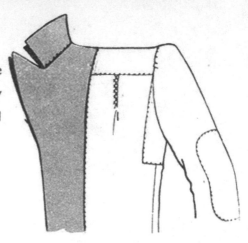

Bind the top of pleat with tape. Cut away the material from the back of box-pleat. This can be used for patching. Then suspend corners from waist band with·tape.

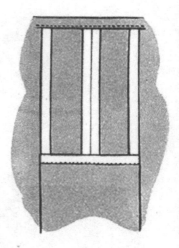

Where the seams meet at the under-arm, tapes can be sewn as shown.

TAPE USED
FOR
STRENGTHENING
PATCH POCKETS
ON THE
WRONG SIDE

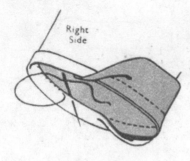

Bind the wrist edge of sleeve with a strip of leather to tone with cloth.

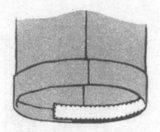

Face the inside of trouser legs with a strip of leather. Place it near the edge at the back where the heel will rub.

Inter-lining applied in this way, on elbows, seats, etc., can easily be removed and replaced when they wear.

F 3854 Wt. 41602 120,120 11 44 Gp. 961 FOSH & CROSS LTD. Ch L.8

Look after your
WOOLLENS
they must last
longer

All woollens, coats, suits, dresses, underwear, blankets, rugs, etc., will last much longer if you take care of them and take advantage of the hints in this leaflet.

MOTHS

The first thing to remember is that it's the grub that eats your clothes, *not* the moth itself. Look out for the little eggs and the white grubs that follow.

Give all woollen clothes a regular airing. Put them on a clothes hanger and let them hang for an hour or so out of doors. Then give them a good brushing or shaking. Look particularly underneath seams, cuffs, revers and turn-ups, and in side pockets.

* * *

Never store away soiled woollen material. The dirt acts like a magnet to moths. Examine all stored woollens from time to time, giving them the airing and brushing described above.

Heat will kill moth eggs, so give your clothes a good pressing from time to time. Use a damp cloth between the iron and the garments, and as you press each section, whip away the cloth, substitute a dry cloth, and re-press to dry out the dampness caused by the first pressing.

* * *

Grit and dust wear away the fibres, so brush and shake all woollen clothes often. Deal with stains at once— warm water removes *most* stains if they are treated immediately.

HOW TO WASH WOOL

NEVER BOIL

Never Boil Woollens—they should never be subjected to extremes of heat and cold, and should not be left wet longer than is absolutely necessary.

Wash quickly in a lather of soapsuds. You don't need a lot of soap if you make sure that it is all completely dissolved. Squeeze woollen garments to remove the dirt—never rub or twist.

NEVER SOAK

Rinse woollens well to make sure no soap is left in them, then dry them as quickly as possible away from artificial heat.

NEVER TWIST

If you are washing hand-knitted garments, treat them with even greater care. NEVER WRING. After rinsing, wrap in a towel, and squeeze to allow the surplus moisture to be absorbed by the towel. Then lay flat, pull to the correct shape, and dry in this position. The ideal way to dry woollens is to lay the garment on a string hammock or on a cloth over a wire tray or on a roller towel fastened to the ends of two chairs.

IRONING. *Press washing woollen fabric materials lightly on the wrong side when they are dry. Knitted clothes don't usually need pressing.*

HINTS ON MENDING AND RE-INFORCING.

All woollen garments should be reinforced on the inside where they get hard wear—if they are new before you start wearing them. This will make them last much longer.

Once they become threadbare or develop a tear or a hole, the best way to mend them is to draw threads of the same material from a seam or hem, and darn with this. Holes can be mended invisibly by cutting a patch from the inside of a hem, as much bigger than the hole as can be managed. Fray the edges of the patch and darn these frayed ends into the material round the hole. If only a small patch can be managed, lay it underneath the hole and darn it with threads drawn from a seam.

Pockets and belts can often be used for patching and mending. Do not bother about matching the material, as it is quite fashionable these days to have patches of contrasting colours.

To refoot knitted socks pick out a stitch with a knitting needle and pull gently to form a loop, then break the thread and gradually withdraw it all along the row. This will separate the foot from the ankle portion. Then pick up the stitches and re-knit.

TO PREVENT UNNECESSARY WEAR

★ *Don't carry a handbag under the arm of a coat or dress.*

★ *Sew a loose flap of odd material to cover the fasteners on the petersham of a skirt—otherwise the hooks catch in underclothes and tear them.*

★ *Sew a narrow strip of strong material inside the legs of trousers and slacks where they rub against shoes.*

ALTERATION IDEAS

With light summer coats, a changeover can often be done by unpicking the facings and revers, adjusting the neckline and seaming the coat up the centre front. The sleeves will probably need taking in a little.

You may have an edge-to-edge summer coat which will not quite join down the front. A narrow panel down the centre front will solve the problem. You may have a frock which has become too worn to be of any use as it is, or a blouse worn under the arms. You will probably be able to get enough material out of this to make the panel.

An old coat that is on the long side can be made into a useful two-piece dress and jacket, providing a fairly long blouse or jumper is available to make a top for the dress. Cut the coat round at hip level, and remove facings from the lower part. Join up the centre front seam and sew this new skirt on to lower edge of the blouse.

Then face lower edge of jacket. The original coat must be cut to correspond with the length of the blouse used, so that the jacket and matching part of the skirt just overlap.

Even if a woollen garment is really badly worn, there is bound to be enough good material left to make a jerkin or waistcoat or even a wool blouse with a knitted yoke and sleeves made from an old unravelled knitted garment.

GETTING THE BEST WEAR OUT OF KNITTED GARMENTS

Mend and darn knitted garments as soon as they need it. If there is a large hole at the elbow of a jersey or the heel of a sock, it is easier to knit a new patch and sew it in, rather than to darn the hole.

Never waste a knitted garment, even though it may be badly shrunk or too ragged to wear. Unpick the seams and then unravel each part of the garment, beginning at the end where the knitting was finished off. This is usually at the neck of the jumper or cardigan, at the top of a sleeve, and so on.

Make the unravelled wool into a skein and swish it round in some warm soapy water. It is a good idea to tie the skeins in at least four places before washing, otherwise it will tie itself into inextricable knots. Rinse well, and lay flat to dry. Then wind into balls in the ordinary way. You may have to break the wool a good many times when unravelling. Don't rejoin with knots, but wait until you knit the wool, then unravel the ends a little and roll two together.

Socks can always be refooted in another colour, and jerseys, jumpers and cardigans look quite smart with contrasting sleeves. Don't hesitate to use dark coloured wools for children's underwear—it's out of date now to use light shades only.

*   *   *

Knit up odd lengths of wool into squares and join them together to make blankets, cot-covers, babies' shawls.

New garments can be knitted up from two colours of old wool. Jumpers with contrasting backs and fronts are very useful if you make the neck reversible.

*   *   *

When elbows begin to wear thin in jumpers and jerseys, it is a good idea to take out the sleeves and reverse them.

Printed for H.M. Stationery Office by W. R. Royle & Son Ltd. 51-4002 B.O.T. 5L.

save fuel

FOOD AND FUEL PLANNING

You are a good housewife. You pride yourself on being economical. And you can say with truth that no food is ever wasted in YOUR kitchen. But (and now search your conscience) can you say the same of — fuel?

COOKING FOR VICTORY
MEANS
COOKING WITH ECONOMY

Whether you have a coal range, a gas-cooker or electric-cooker, there is one golden rule for saving fuel— and that is PLAN YOUR MEALS AS FAR AHEAD AS POSSIBLE. Not easy, you say. Agreed, under wartime conditions, what with food rationing and several members of the family on different war jobs, coming home at different times for meals. But when you think of the sacrifices made by our fighting men, isn't it worth the little extra trouble if it means you are helping to bring Victory nearer?

On those days when you are not putting on your oven yet want a hot meal, plan the menu carefully to make the fullest use of your electric hot-plate or gas burner. A tiered steamer is the best answer to the problem. With a little ingenuity you can cook a whole meal—steak pudding, vegetables, and a sweet —over one ring. If you haven't a steamer, improvise with a colander fitted into a saucepan—and fish can be cooked between two plates placed on top.

STEAMERS

FUEL'S MORE PRECIOUS THAN JEWELS....

DON'T DROWN YOUR VEGETABLES

In other words, don't use more water than necessary. This is responsible for a big waste of fuel and the loss of valuable *"Just wallowing"* vitamins. The sight of a large whole cabbage or cauliflower just wallowing in boiling water should not be seen in any kitchen. Remember that the more water you boil the more fuel you are burning. Shred cabbages, break cauliflowers into sprigs, and slice root vegetables into small pieces ; and then try cooking them the quick way—in the minimum quantity of water.

KEEP THE LIDS ON YOUR SAUCEPANS

 This is most important. It takes 15% less gas to bring food to the boil in a covered pan, so the extra care is worth while, don't you think ?

BUTTERED TOAST—OR BULLETS

Of course you like your slice of toast at breakfast. But toast is a dangerous "fuel thief". You would hardly believe it but if *one household* gave up toast for a year there would be 2,000 extra bullets for the war effort. Makes you think, doesn't it ?

ABOUT YOUR GRILLER....

If you have an electric griller, use it rather than your frying pan—and so save fuel. If you cook with gas, do just the opposite ; fry. In either case be sure to make use of the heat above the grill as well as below.

YOUR CUP OF TEA....

Rationing has cut down those cups of tea. Which means that this in itself has helped the fuel problem. Nevertheless, you can still make tea in the *economical* way. For example, never boil more water than is needed. A half-filled kettle comes to the boil in far less time than a full one—and thus saves time as well as fuel.

SAVING YOUR BIT....

 Well, we have given you here only a few fuel-saving hints—there are plenty more, of course —but if you act on these alone you will be making a real and valuable contribution to Victory. For just as every fighting man can say "I am doing my bit", so every housewife who cuts out cooking-fuel waste can say with justifiable pride : "I have *saved* my bit".

SAVE FUEL FOR WINTER WARMTH

F.3315 Wt.27393 400,000 8/44 Gp.961 Fosh & Cross, Ltd.

Easy to make slippers for the whole family

★ Slippers save a lot of wear and tear on outdoor shoes in the house, and can be made quite easily at home. You'll probably have enough materials for them among the pieces in your rag-bag. Here are full instructions.

making the soles . . . Materials : leather, cardboard, canvas, rope, string, rug wool, old carpet, macrame twine, old stockings cut into strips and plaited.

Getting the size : put feet flat on paper and trace the outlines, cut out patterns for both feet, marking right and left carefully.

Making up : Fabric or leather soles—if using woollen material, cut each sole 4 times. But don't forget, the thicker and stronger the sole, the longer it will wear. Stitch pieces together across and across until quilted all over (diagram 1). Leave $\frac{1}{4}$ in. all round for welt on which to sew the uppers.

Dia. 1

Dia. 2

For plaited-stocking, rope, string, etc., soles : Cut out one sole for each foot in canvas or other strong material, allowing ¼ in. turnings. Using strong darning or carpet needle and linen thread or fine twine, stab stitch plait to canvas, beginning at A (diagram 2). Go right through, and sew each strand to the next strand. Fill up sole until only ¼ in. welt is left. Sew end of plait flat on top of sole. This type of sole needs an inner sole.

uppers . . . Materials for outer covers : silk, satin, lace, woollen materials, cretonne, tapestry, old felt hats, curtaining, yarn wool, rug wool, fur, fur fabric, velvet, velveteen, leather, old carpet. For linings : old underwear, silk, velvet, velveteen, fur, fur cloth and coat interlinings.

Interlinings : should be of strong, stiffish materials such as canvas, old deck-chair canvas, old fine-straw hats, stout cotton. It is very important to put some kind of stiffening in the heels ; otherwise they soon get trodden down.

welting the upper to the sole . . .

To stitch uppers to sole, use two needles, and strong waxed thread. Insert needles into same hole, one up and one down (diagram 3). Pull stitches tightly and try to make them even.

Dia 3

CHILD'S RUG WOOL SLIPPER *size 10*

soles . . . Leather or made-up sole. See previous directions.

making uppers . . . when casting on put needle behind instead of through stitches. This makes a firm edge so that there is no need to knit into the back of stitches in first row.

Cast on 46 sts. with No. 5 needles. *1st row* : knit to end. *2nd row* : knit to end. *3rd row* : knit to end. *4th row* : decrease once at each end of row by knitting 2 tog. *5th row* : knit to end. Repeat 4th and 5th rows until 38 sts. remain on needle. *12th row* : decrease once at each end. *13th row* : decrease once at each end. Repeat 12th and 13th rows until 26 sts. remain on needle. Cast off.

This completes the shaping of the upper. Join ends. Press. Measurements when finished : length at top 10 in., at bottom 16 in., depth 3½ in. Oversew the lower edge to sole.

Quickly made, warm and strong. To make a larger size cast on 2 extra stitches for each increase in shoe size.

BABY'S CROCHET SHOE *2 years*

Material required : Soft cotton yarn.

upper . . . *1st row :* Chain 71. *2nd row :* 69 DC. Repeat 2nd row 3 times. *6th row :* Miss 1 DC, DC along row until 2 remain, miss 1 DC, DC into last st. *7th row :* Miss 2 DC, DC along row until 3 remain, miss 2 DC, 1 DC into last st. Repeat 6th and 7th rows until 45 DC are left. *14th row :* Miss 1 DC each end of every row until 37 DC are left. *18th row :* Work without decreasing. Repeat 18th row twice more.
Measurement when finished : length of top 5 in., length of bottom 10 in., depth 2⅛ in.

sole . . . *1st row :* 18 chain. DC into each chain and turn at end. DC back into each chain on other side. Continue for 5 rounds, increasing at each end to keep work flat. Slip stitch 7 sts. at each side for instep in next round and continue in DC for 4 rounds, still slipping the 7 sts. This completes the heel and instep. For the

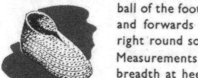

ball of the foot, turn at instep, and DC backwards and forwards round toe for 2 rows. DC once right round sole to finish. Press.
Measurements when finished : length 5 in., breadth at heel 2 in., at ball of foot 2½ in.

making up . . . Stitch up front of uppers to within top 5 rows. Press. Stitch uppers to edge of sole.

SLIPPERS FOR MEN AND WOMEN

Materials required : outside covering, inter-lining, lining, braid. Leather or made-up sole—see previous directions.
Patterns given to scale for size 8 and 5.

cutting out . . . For men's slippers, follow outer line of diagram. For women's follow inner line. Allow ¼ in. turnings. *For each foot*, cut heel-pieces twice and toe-pieces once, in all materials. Cut out sole in lining once, if required.

making up . . . Begin by joining centre-back seam A-B of all heel-pieces (diagram 4). Then assemble pieces of entire shoe, placing outer covers and linings wrong sides facing, with interlining in between. Stitch heel-pieces together to within ¼ in. of outside

edges. Bind upper edges A-C with strong braid. Match B of heel
to B of sole (diagram 5) and oversew firmly. Stitch toe-pieces together
in the same way. Match F of toe (diagram 6) to F of sole (diagram 5).
Oversew, easing in round top of toe. Place heel-piece inside toe-
piece at C-C. Sew overlap securely. Now take braid and welt it
over sole and uppers so that $\frac{1}{4}$ in. welt is left all round (diagram 3,
page 2). Try on slipper, and adjust upper edge of heel to toe, at the
overlap according to the fit of the foot, and sew firmly. If bought
sole is used bind edges C-B-C and D-F-E before welting on to sole.

*　　　*　　　*　　　*　　　*　　　*

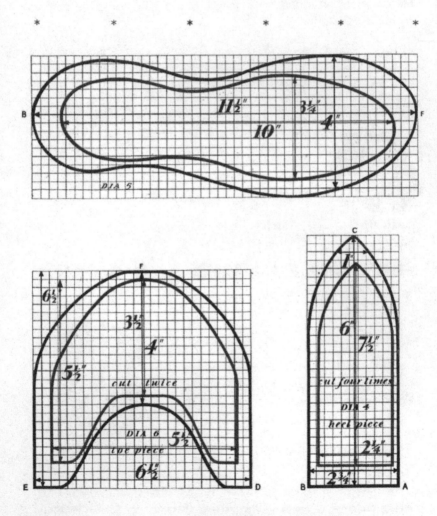

HOW TO PATCH A SHIRT

by

Mrs. SEW-and-SEW

● Shirts are easy to mend, as the patches can be cut from other parts of the garment. They can be replaced by similar material cut from a discarded shirt, or soft cotton. When the cuffs start to fray, they should be carefully unpicked and reversed. As they are double, the worn edge will then be inside the fold. If you are using new fabric for patching, it should be washed first.

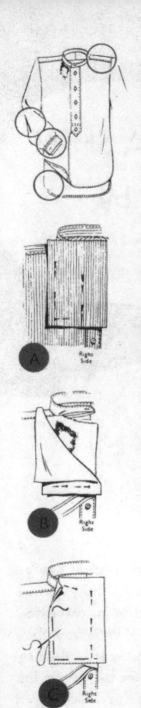

Parts indicated by circles can be used for patches. The sleeves can be cut short for summer wear

A Cut patch to extend well over neck-band, yoke and front hem

B Unpick neck-band and front hem, and pin patch in position. Match pattern exactly

C Tack patch firmly, folding $\frac{1}{4}''$ turning along straight edges and hem neatly

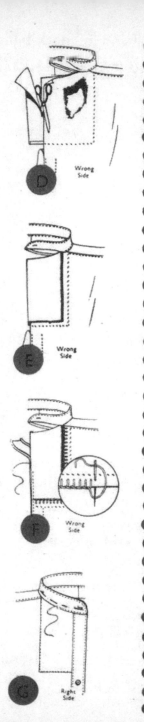

D Turn to wrong side and trim to shape of neck and front

E Then cut away worn part of shirt leaving $\frac{1}{4}''$ turning from the hemming stitches

F Blanket-stitch the turnings and sew front hem back into position

G Turn back to right side and tack and stitch top layer of neck-band by machine

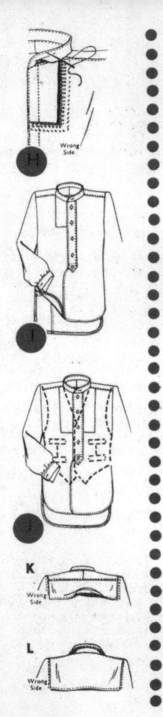

H Hem lining of neck-band down and this completes the patch

I This illustration shows the piece replaced in the lower corner of tail

J If patch does not match shirt, patch both fronts to extend below the neck edge of waistcoat

K Strengthening back of shirt, by inserting extra piece into yoke and sleeves

L Strengthening back of pyjama coat, by inserting yoke at shoulders

F.3500 Wt. 36067 100,000 10/44 Gp. 961 Fosh & Cross Ltd.
Ch L—1

TOO HOT AN IRON IS DANGEROUS

After washing, nylon should be dried by laying it out flat. If this is done, you will find little need to iron it at all. But if you do decide the garment needs pressing, make this test: stand your iron on a newspaper for 15-20 seconds. If the paper scorches, the iron is too hot. Give it time to cool!

Nylon can be ironed on either side—only one thickness at a time, if possible. Take great care not to press buttons or fastenings into the fabric, and not to crease it in any way. Damp the fabric if it gets too dry.

DRESSMAKING WITH NYLON

Allow ample material so as not to strain the seams, and never make the garment too close-fitting. This nylon fabric is rather apt to slip at the seams. So make liberal turnings at seams and hems, and always tack very carefully before you start to sew. Set your machine at as low tension as possible. By machining with a loose, easy stitch, you will avoid puckering at the seams.

You can send nylon to the laundry if you wish. They know how to handle it.

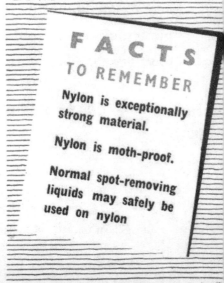

FACTS
TO REMEMBER

Nylon is exceptionally strong material.

Nylon is moth-proof.

Normal spot-removing liquids may safely be used on nylon

A5200 Wt.42881 100,000 1/46 Gp.961 Fosh & Cross Ltd., Londo

How to look after Parachute Nylon

The nylon appearing in the shops at the moment is parachute nylon, so don't expect all the advantages next year's nylon will offer.

THIS IS HOW TO WASH NYLON

Use warm water and dissolve the soap thoroughly. Rinse repeatedly to remove all trace of suds. You may rub or wring the fabric, but it is not advisable to twist it. As nylon fabric dries very quickly, it is an advantage to iron it as soon as possible after washing.

In the case of coloured goods, be sure that the colours are fast. If they are inclined to run, wash the garment by itself.

SOME USEFUL HINTS FOR REPAIRING MEN'S AND BOYS' CLOTHES

Smarten up - your men!

says Mrs. SEW-and-SEW

There's nothing more necessary in these days than knowing how to keep your husband's and boys' clothes neat and in good repair. They are as easy to mend as your own if you only know the right way to set about it. This leaflet gives you some tailor's ways of patching coats, trousers and shirts. But if you have any problems, take them straight to a Make-Do and Mend Class and get expert advice.

SUITS AND RAINCOATS

TO CLEAN GREASY COLLARS AND CUFFS : Brush well with 1 table-spoonful of ammonia to a pint of water. Scrub gently if very dirty.

TO SAVE WEAR ON CUFFS, COLLARS AND ELBOWS : Reinforce with patches or bindings of leather. Easy to sew and looks tidy and smart.

KEEP YOUR SOCKS IN WEAR

TO REINFORCE WHILE NEW : *Hand-knit:* Darn toes and heels. Or, knit another strand of fine wool at heels and toes. *Machine-knit:* Darn before wearing with fine soft cotton or fine wool.

TO MEND STRONGLY : Always use fine wool, make rows of stitches close and even, darn well beyond worn place inside sock, leaving loops at the ends of each row.

TO RE-FOOT HAND-KNIT SOCKS : Unpick welt if you have no spare wool to match, using it to re-knit heels and toes or foot. Knit on new welt, of quiet colour contrast for men, and bold gay contrast for children. This is a good way to use up left-over knitting wool.

TO RE-FOOT MACHINE-KNIT SOCKS : Cut off old felted foot and use as pattern for cutting new foot from another old pair. Machine or backstitch to leg. Open seam and herringbone edges of seam quite flat to sock. Keep stitching loose.

ISSUED BY THE   BOARD OF TRADE

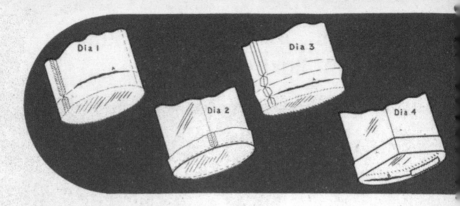

TROUSERS

TO KEEP BRACES BUTTONS FROM TEARING AWAY : Reinforce waistband inside with soft leather, and sew on the buttons right through the leather. Or sew a tab of leather behind each button.

TO SAVE WEAR ON TROUSER ENDS : Sew a strip of leather inside turn-ups at heel.

TO MEND FRAYED TROUSER ENDS—*Without turn-ups:* Unpick hemming, let down, press material. As Diagram (1) showing worn part at (A), reverse hem, right side to right side, sew off a small seam—Diagram (2) —slightly larger than the frayed part at (B). Refold hem back on to the inside, hem and press. The same diagrams and method could serve also for a frayed jacket or shirt sleeve cuff. *Trousers with turn-ups :* Unpick hemming, let down turn-up, and press material. Diagram (3) worn part now showing at (A). Refold turn-up slightly narrower than before and tack into position as Diagram (4). This allows a slightly wider hem and carries frayed portion on to the inside as at (B) cover fray with binding.

TO RENEW POCKETS STRONGLY WITHOUT UNPICKING : Cut worn pocket 1 in. away from where it is sewn into the trouser. Cut out a

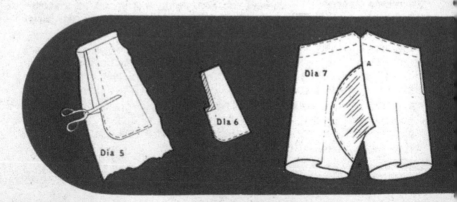

new pocket like the old one, allowing for turnings. Seam sides and bottom. Make one turning on top of pocket, tack to inch of remaining material, hem or machine. Turn pocket inside out, turn in the other raw edge and hem down. This gives a strong wide double seam. A jacket pocket can be renewed in this way too. (Diagrams 5 and 6).

TO RE-SEAT TROUSERS : Unpick seat and leg seams from point (A) to point (B) see diagram (7). Cut two new seat pieces, to size and shape required (see diagram) but large enough to extend 1 in. beyond worn part. Turn and stitch down curved edge to trousers and remake seat and leg seams, making certain that the seat piece is included in the seaming.

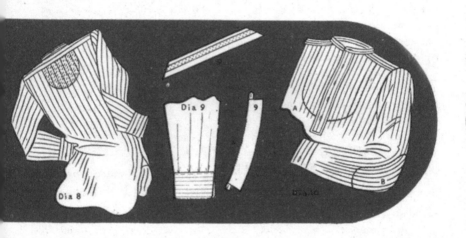

FOUR GOOD HINTS FOR SHIRTS

TO REPAIR SHABBY COLLARS AND CUFFS : Tuck in frayed edges and stitch new folds together. For double cuffs and collars, stitch tape over worn part, and reverse so that tape comes underneath (Diagram 9).

TO MEND WORN SHIRT FRONTS : Cut patches of same size and shape from tail or underneath part of yoke. Set edges of patches into yoke seam, and neck-band and into the stitching of front fastening (Diagram 10A). Replace tail with other washing material.

TO REPAIR "BRACES" WEAR AT BACK : Put patch over worn place, setting it into yoke. Cut nothing away, but stitch across and across, double thickness. (Diagram 8).

TO REPAIR SLEEVES : Cut all sleeve patches really large. Patch on right side, matching material. (Diagram 10B).

CARDIGANS AND JERSEYS

TO REINFORCE WHEN NEW : Use the same method as for socks.

TO REPAIR : Use the same method as for socks. But for thick jerseys, try "Swiss" darning (Diagram 11). For this, work on right side, with fine matching wool, following the loops of the knitting, and using a wool needle or the eye of a darning needle. Run the wool out on the wrong side when finished.

TO REPAIR HAND-KNITS : Use the knitted patch method. Pick up stitches ½ in. beyond thin place or hole with fine knitting needle. Knit patch of right size, allowing ½ in. extra. Graft in last row of stitches, or cast off and hem down. Darn thin place to patch. Hem down sides of patch and press under damp cloth. (Made either on the right or wrong side, this patch is almost invisible.) It can be used for socks, too. (Diagram 12). You can get matching wool for these repairs by unpicking welt at waist and wrists, and knitting new welts as for socks.

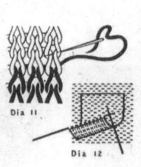

Dia 11

Dia 12

VESTS, PANTS AND PYJAMAS

TO DARN STOCKINETTE VESTS AND PANTS : Use soft cotton mending thread or fine wool, darning well beyond worn patch.

TO DARN CELLULAR COTTON : Use soft mending cotton—or patch on right side.

TO PATCH PYJAMAS : Patch on right side, using old pockets for patches if you have no pieces.

At your service !

F.3796 Wt.38511 120,000 5/45 Gp.961 Fosh & Cross Ltd., London B.O.T. 12 L.

"Never send a Hole to the wash"

advises Mrs. SEW-and-SEW

EMERGENCY MEND FOR SHEET OR PILLOW CASE

STORAGE

If you have some linen not in use, store it away—but not in a hot cupboard and not if it is starched. For long storage wrap in paper parcels—and place in a cool, dry, chest, cupboard or drawer. Wash, mend and air before putting away. Refold at intervals to prevent wear at the creases. Only store clean linen.

MENDING

There is a lot of wear left in linens which look worn and every ounce of wear must be got out of them. Hold sheets, pillowcases and towels up to a strong light and look through them—this will often show up tiny holes and slits—such as cuts made by razor blades, which are almost invisible before the towel is washed, but become large ragged tears afterwards. Be sure that if pillowcase buttons are hanging loose they are taken off before sending it to the wash.

When patching use old material—a new patch on a worn towel for instance is liable to tear it away. Always mend linen before it is washed—if you haven't time to do so properly, draw it together roughly for the time being with an oversewing stitch. Thin spots should be reinforced by darning, either by hand or machine before they actually wear into holes. A two-sided tear should be darned in both directions, so that the place of the tear is doubly darned.

SHEETS AND PILLOW CASES

When sheets get very thin, turn them sides to middle by cutting them lengthways down the centre, and either over-sewing the outside selvedges together or joining them with a run and fell seam. Trim away the torn parts of what are now the sides of the sheet. Turn in the edges and hem them.

If a sheet already turned sides-to-middle has become too thin to use, wait until you have another one in the same condition, then join the two together. Place them smoothly one on top of the other, then sew them together down the centre with a row of running stitches. To prevent uncomfortable wrinkles, the sheets must be " locked " together. Do this by smoothing the two from the stitching outwards, then running another line of stitching down the sheet parallel with the first line. Do the same on the other side, spacing the lines of stitching about 12 in. apart until the sides are reached. Oversew the outside edges of the sheets together and darn any small holes or thin patches through both thicknesses of material.

One fair sized sheet can be made to do the work of two by cutting a line about 18 in. long down the centre of the top—these edges should be hemmed. The sheet can then be used double on a small bed, the slit allowing the top to be turned back over the blankets without difficulty.

Hemstitched borders on sheets or pillowcases can be mended by tacking the two edges on to strong paper, leaving a narrow channel between, and joining the two with faggot stitch. The simplest form of faggot stitch is just a bar with the thread twisted round it.

When pillowcases get too thin to be used without risk of tearing, join the front and back together with rows of running stitching as in the illustration—then add a false back of any washing material, and slip in the pillow in the ordinary way.

Bolster cases are not essential now-a-days—the bolster can be covered with the lower sheet. If you are short of pillowcases unpick the seam that runs the length of the bolster, fold the material over, so that the two ends come together, and rejoin the two sides to form a pillow-case.

TOWELS

Thin places and small holes can be reinforced by machine darning or by hand darning with soft mending cotton.

Large holes should be patched with the sound parts of other old towelling—never use new material. Patches on towels should be tacked in position without the edges of the patch being turned in. These edges should then be stitched on to the towel with herringbone or cross-stitch. If you haven't a towel rail, fix a loop to two diagonal corners of the towel so that it can be hung up without being damaged—change the loop it is hanging on from time to time—this will equalize wear—as towels are bound to be used while they are hanging on a hook. Sew two thin tea towels together, arranging that the holes in the one are covered with the sound part of the other cloth.

When dusters wear thin, sew two together round the edge and several times across the centre.

B.O.T. 17 L.   A 4541 Wt. 60155   200,000 4/45 Gp. 961 Fosh & Cross Ltd., London.

Patches are **important**—every one you put on helps you to put off buying something new.   And it's just as easy to patch properly as to cobble.   Half the battle is knowing how to cut and place your material.   Here are some hints to help you—and remember that reinforcing garments while they are new will save you much patching later on.

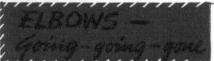

A two-seam sleeve that's worn through at the elbow can best be repaired by putting in a new section, if you have sufficient matching material available.

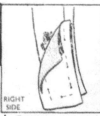

1 Cut patch to extend well beyond hole, seams and cuff. Pin in place on right side.

2 Unpick lining and seams to the top level of patch.

3 Sew Patch on above hole by placing right sides together to give a flat pressed seam on the wrong side.

4 Trim new section to the shape of the worn sleeve and cut away worn part.

5 Machine the sleeve side seams, notch and press them open. Catch-stitch turning at wrist.

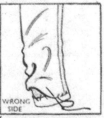

6 Replace lining and hem lower edge to wrist.

★ New coats and knickers can be strengthened before wearing by patching neatly on the wrong side.

When a Garment 'GOES' UNDERARM

Circles on the diagram at left suggest where material for patches may be cut away from the lining of the yoke, or by removing pocket, belt, cuffs, collar or hem lining. Where necessary, replace with a contrasting material.

I Cut patch to extend well over arm-hole and side seam. Match pattern carefully.

Cloth Knickers call for Neatness

The first step is to unpick central back seam and part of inner leg seams (1). Use a round patch in two pieces cut to shape of both leg seams (2). Do not cut away the worn part, as this helps to reinforce the new patch.

Rescue Work on Coat Lining

Diagram (1) shows how to shape patches to renew the underarm lining in a coat. The armhole seam must be undone to allow these to be put in place.

WRONG SIDE

TO R... PAT...

1 Patch ... part rou... well as the...

2 Selvedge ... tern of patch ... those of the ga...

3 Patches must no... over hems or seam ... must first be un... patch put on and new ... or seam stitched on to pa...

Saving a Shirt

Pieces for patches can be taken from the tail of the shirt and replaced there by any soft cotton. If new material is used it should be washed first.

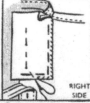

I Cut patch to extend well over, neckband yoke and front hem.

2 Unpick neckband and front hem and pin patch in position, taking care to match pattern exactly.

3 Tack patch firmly, folding ⅛ in. turning along straight edges. Hem neatly.

4 Turn to wrong side and trim to shape of neck and front.

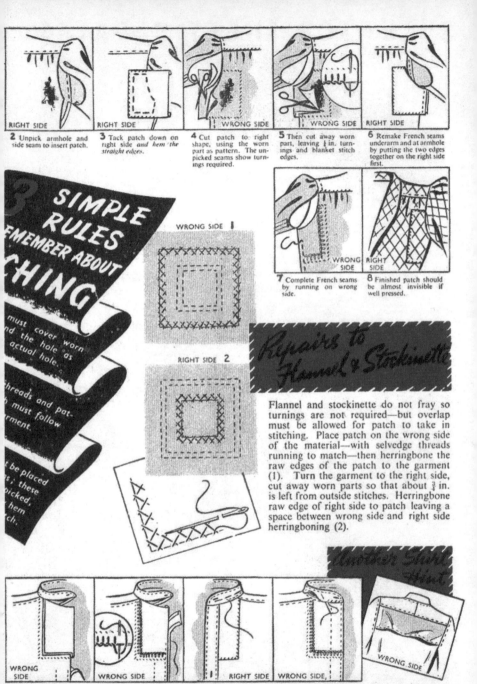

RIGHT SIDE — **2** Unpick armhole and side seam to insert patch.

RIGHT SIDE — **3** Tack patch down on right side *and hem the straight edges.*

WRONG SIDE — **4** Cut patch to right shape, using the worn part as pattern. The unpicked seams show turnings required.

WRONG SIDE — **5** Then cut away worn part, leaving ¼ in. turnings and blanket stitch edges.

RIGHT SIDE — **6** Remake French seams underarm and at armhole by putting the two edges together on the right side first.

WRONG SIDE / RIGHT SIDE — **7** Complete French seams by running on wrong side.

8 Finished patch should be almost invisible if well pressed.

3 SIMPLE RULES TO REMEMBER ABOUT ~CHING

... must cover worn ... and the hole as ... actual hole.

... reads and pat- ... must follow ... ment.

... be placed ... s; these ... picked, ... hem ... ch.

WRONG SIDE **1**

RIGHT SIDE **2**

Repairs to Flannel & Stockinette

Flannel and stockinette do not fray so turnings are not required—but overlap must be allowed for patch to take in stitching. Place patch on the wrong side of the material—with selvedge threads running to match—then herringbone the raw edges of the patch to the garment (1). Turn the garment to the right side, cut away worn parts so that about ⅜ in. is left from outside stitches. Herringbone raw edge of right side to patch leaving a space between wrong side and right side herringboning (2).

Another Shirt Hint

WRONG SIDE — **5** Cut away worn part of shirt, leaving ¼ in. turning from hemming stitches.

WRONG SIDE — **6** Blanket-stitch the turnings and tack and sew front hem back into position.

RIGHT SIDE — **7** Turn back to right side and tack and stitch top layer of neckband by machine.

WRONG SIDE — **8** Hem down lining of neckband. This completes the patch.

WRONG SIDE — **9** To strengthen the back of a shirt, insert an extra thickness at yoke.

RULES FOR SHEET REPAIRS

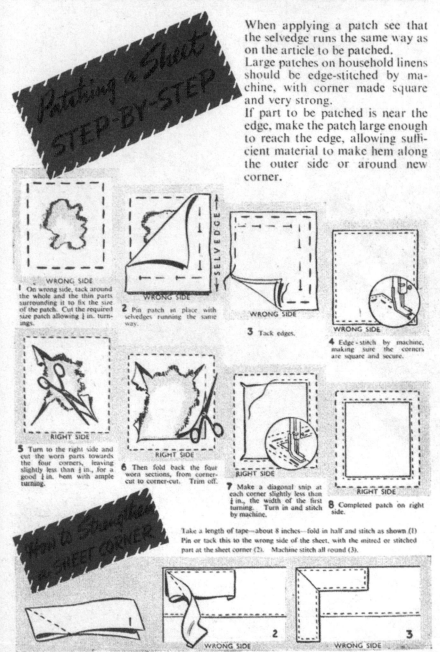

Putting a Sheet STEP-BY-STEP

When applying a patch see that the selvedge runs the same way as on the article to be patched.

Large patches on household linens should be edge-stitched by machine, with corner made square and very strong.

If part to be patched is near the edge, make the patch large enough to reach the edge, allowing sufficient material to make hem along the outer side or around new corner.

WRONG SIDE

1 On wrong side, tack around the whole and the thin parts surrounding it to fix the size of the patch. Cut the required size patch allowing ¼ in. turnings.

WRONG SIDE — SELVEDGE

2 Pin patch in place with selvedges running the same way.

WRONG SIDE

3 Tack edges.

WRONG SIDE

4 Edge-stitch by machine, making sure the corners are square and secure.

RIGHT SIDE

5 Turn to the right side and cut the worn parts towards the four corners, leaving slightly less than ¼ in., for a good ¼ in. hem with ample turning.

RIGHT SIDE

6 Then fold back the four worn sections, from corner-cut to corner-cut. Trim off.

RIGHT SIDE

7 Make a diagonal snip at each corner slightly less than ¼ in., the width of the first turning. Turn in and stitch by machine.

RIGHT SIDE

8 Completed patch on right side.

How to Strengthen a SHEET CORNER

Take a length of tape—about 8 inches—fold in half and stitch as shown (1) Pin or tack this to the wrong side of the sheet, with the mitred or stitched part at the sheet corner (2). Machine stitch all round (3).

1

2 WRONG SIDE

3 WRONG SIDE

Printed for H.M. Stationery Office by C.&Co., London, S.E.1.   51-1612

B.O.T. 7.L

Hints on Renovating and Recutting!

"THINK BEFORE YOU CUT"

Says Mrs. Sew - and - Sew

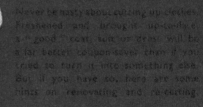

Never be hasty about cutting up clothes. Freshened and brought up-to-date, a "good" coat, suit or dress will be a far better coupon-saver than if you tried to turn it into something else. But if you have to, here are some hints on renovating and re-cutting.

"REFRESHERS" FOR COATS, SUITS AND DRESSES

Hand brushing and thorough sponging and pressing is the finest tonic for good cloth.

All grease marks (especially round the neck) should be removed first either with warm water and ammonia (1 tablespoonful to 1 pint) or with proprietary cleaning fluid.

Then you can consider :—

1 Renewing old trimmings ; removing shabby fur collars.

2 Altering neck-lines, and adding new collars and cuffs of contrasting material.

3 Getting a new length of stuff and giving dresses entirely new fronts, sleeves or half-sleeves.

4 Relining—and for boys' and men's jackets—binding with leather.

ISSUED BY THE BOARD OF TRADE

SIMPLE RULES FOR RE-CUTTING

Remember :—

Even large clothes, when unpicked, cannot be cut and re-made into clothes the same size. If the style is made up of many pieces, or cut on the cross, you will probably only be able to get a blouse, blousette, or small children's clothes out of it

Before you start look at the article carefully and mark all the worn places, moth holes, tears, stains and pocket positions with tacking thread—this will remind you to avoid them when cutting.

Choosing your pattern. Simplicity is the secret of success. Choose a pattern which takes little material, is not cut on the cross and has few pieces. For instance, if you plan to make a blouse out of an old dress—don't attempt a fussy style. Select a simple shirt and you're far more likely to be pleased with the result.

Preparing your material. Unpick carefully.

Tools needed for unpicking : Sharp razor-blade, with which you must be very careful. Pen-knife or small sharp-pointed scissors.

How to unpick : Take off buttons, snaps, etc., unpick collar, cuffs, trimmings, etc. Take out sleeves and any linings, let down hem and unpick large main seams, take off seam bindings, let out pleats, gathers or darts. Always pull out stitching threads as you unpick, and unpick "neatening" of turnings to preserve their full width. This often makes all the difference between skimping the new garment and getting the new pattern pieces cut with room to spare.

Cleaning and freshening. Wash after unpicking. That is a safe rule. Washing takes out stitch marks and gives the stuff back a lot of life and spring. If the garment has been recently washed or cleaned, simply sponge with ammonia and water (1 tablespoonful to 1 pint) and press. If it is dirty proceed as follows :—Shake out all dust, outdoors if possible. Scrape off fluff with back of knife or bone paper-knife from inside of hem, pleats and seams. Wash material in warm suds and rinse thoroughly. Take out any stains that are left.

Before cutting your pattern read the directions on the pattern envelope carefully. Hold up your unpicked pieces of material to the light and mark the worn places with tailor's chalk or tack marks, and this will remind you to avoid them. If this is not possible try and place them in the new garment where they get the least wear. Cut out a whole pattern of fronts, backs and both sleeves in paper. You will find this is a great help. It saves time in placing the pattern—you can see at a glance that you have enough material and haven't left any piece uncut.

Placing your pattern. Spread all the pieces of the new pattern out on your unpicked material. Make sure that the run of the thread, weave and nap is the right way for the new style. Pin each piece and mark all notches, darts, etc., by tailor's tackings. Never put scissors to the material until all the pattern pieces have been planned, pinned and plainly marked by tailor's tackings or chalk marks.

SOME DRESSMAKER METHODS AND ESSENTIAL STITCHES

OPEN SEAM

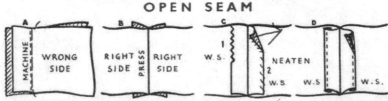

★ *This is a joining seam, and is used for nearly all materials. It is unsuited for thin materials which fray readily. Place the two right sides together, and tack about ½″ from the edges ; then machine. See Diagram A ; open seam and press flat. See Diagram B ; neaten edges as follows : 1. Pinking. With sharp scissors cut " V " gashes all along the edge of each seam. See Diagram C.1 ; 2. Overcast. Turn in edge of seam and put your needle under the edge and out on top of folded edge all along seam. Work loosely from right to left. See Diagram C.2 ; 3. Turn under edges and machine taking care not to stitch the garment as well. See Diagram D. All these finishing methods are used only on the raw edges of the seams.*

SHAM SLOT OR STITCHED SEAM

★ *Place right sides of material together, tack about ½″ from edges and machine. See Diagram A ; open seam and press flat. Turn to right side and machine up each side of the join. See Diagram B ; on the wrong side of the material, neaten seam edges by overcasting edges. See Diagram C.*

MACHINED FOLD HEM

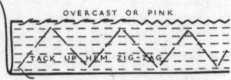

OVERCAST OR PINK

TACK UP HEM ZIG-ZAG

★ Tack up your hem with zig-zag stitches to required depth. See Diagram ; machine several times round hem, placing the first row of machining near the folded edge and then spacing the following rows evenly ; overcast or pink edges. Do not set the machine tension too tightly ; this is a useful hem for children's clothes which are being let down.

"FRENCH BIND" HEM

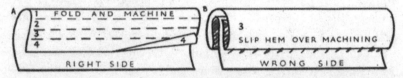

A
1
2
3
4
FOLD AND MACHINE
RIGHT SIDE

B
3.
SLIP HEM OVER MACHINING
WRONG SIDE

★ You will need to fold over on the right side of your material, 4 times the width of the material you require for your finished bind, e.g., if the bind when finished is to be ¼" then fold back 1" ; machine along line 1. See Diagram A ; turn over material and press up over stitching. Now turn the raw edge under at line 3. See Diagram A ; bring fold over to wrong side of garment. Slip hem the fold to the machine stitching. See Diagram B.

REGULATION PLACKET

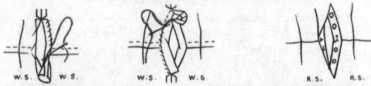

W.S.   W.S.   W.S.   W.S.   R.S.   R.S.

★ Snip seam across below and above opening. Finish front edge of side opening with a bias facing ½" wide. (See Diagram I) ; slip hem to garment. Finish back hedge with a straight fold of material 1" wide. Machine right sides together. Fold back material with ¼" hem and slip-stitch to line of machining. (See Diagram 2) ; put a hook and eye at the waist line and snaps above and below. (See Diagram 3.)

A QUICKLY MADE PLACKET

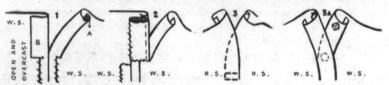

W.S.   1   2   3   3A
OPEN AND OVERCAST   B
W.S. W.S.   W.S.   R.S. R.S.   W.S.   W.S.

★ Allow wider turnings on the seams at the place for the opening. Seam to the end of the opening. Open seam and press. Fold under at A. (See Diagram I) and turn back hem in line with seam, and slip stitch down. Snip across at B. (See Diagram I) ; put in an extra piece of cloth right side to right side of the garment, so that it laps under part A of placket (see Diagram 2) ; machine these edges together, and fold back on wrong side ; then slip stitch as in Diagram 2. Close the placket and stitch across lower end (2 rows) to keep the end secure and stop the breaking of seams. (See Diagrams 3 and 3a.)

Remember the placket always fastens from right to left on women's and girl's garments.

F4416 Wt. 55458 120,120 3,45 Gp. 961 Fosh & Cross Ltd., London.   B.O.T. 13L

Darning

DO's AND DON'Ts

A neat darn is a real badge of honour these days—and, done in good time, it can lengthen the life of a garment by months and months. Here are some hints on everyday darns and how to set about them; with some general rules for your guidance.

Do *darn on the wrong side directly a thin place appears.*
- *tack a piece of net on a large hole and darn across it for extra strength (see linen darn)*
- *darn well beyond the weak place.*
- *leave loops at the turns to allow for shrinking.*
- *settle yourself comfortably in a good light before you start.*

Don't *wait for a hole to develop.*
use thread too coarse or too fine
- *make straight edges to your darn; a little irregularity distributes the strain.*
- *pull the thread taut or it will pucker.*
- *expect to make a success of a job by hit-or-miss methods.*

To darn a Hole

A. Weave the needle in and out to make a darn of an irregular diamond shape, working well beyond the thin area surrounding the hole.

B. Turn darn round and work across the hole in the opposite direction, remembering to leave tiny loops at the end of each line of stitching and to weave in and out of the first strands across the hole.

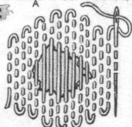
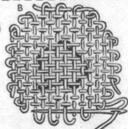

To darn a tear

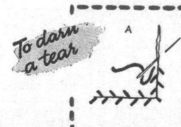
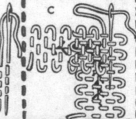

A. First tack a piece of paper behind the tear, to hold edges in position. Then fish-bone stitch the edges of the tear together. Use fine thread of same colour.

B. Take darning stitches well beyond tear, right across base, forming a rectangle.

C. Turn work round and darn in the same way across the other part of the tear. A solid square will be formed at the corner. Now remove tacking thread and paper.

To darn a Knitted Fabric

For the first stages, see 'To darn a Hole' (a) overleaf. But when you turn the darn, take the second set of stitches in a diagonal direction as shewn above.

To join Locknit Seams

Work buttonhole stitch along each side and then sew the knots of the buttonholing together. This method is suitable, too, for mending straight tears in a glove, a suede jacket or a fur coat, as it lessens the strain on the material.

To repair torn Buttonholes

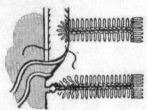

Usually it is the outer edges of buttonholes that 'go.' To tidy and strengthen them, stitch a length of tape or a narrow band of matching material along the edge of the garment. Then re-do the buttonholing over the new material (Diagram).

To darn a Slit

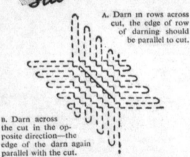

A. Darn in rows across cut, the edge of row of darning should be parallel to cut.

B. Darn across the cut in the opposite direction—the edge of the darn again parallel with the cut.

To darn a Stocking Ladder

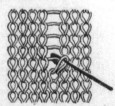

Work on the right side and use a fine steel crochet hook. Place it into a dropped loop and draw the straight thread above it through the loop. Repeat as necessary. Have a needle ready threaded, darn in from above ladder and towards it. Pass needle through the crocheted loop and darn back to start. Bring up any further runs in the ladder and finish off in the same way.

To darn Linen

A particularly neat and easy darn can be made on articles which are used only right side up, such as pillowcases, table cloths and table napkins, by lightly tacking a scrap of net over the hole on the wrong side, and darning in and out of it on the right side. Trim away the surplus edges on the wrong side after darning. This type of darn can be used for any kind of plain material where invisible mending is not essential.

RIGHT SIDE

WRONG SIDE

Printed for H.M. Stationery Office by Sellar & Sellar Ltd., Hayes, Middx. 51-4633

Fuel sense saves money in the home

65 EASY WAYS OF SAVING MONEY

YOUR FUEL SENSE

means more pennies in your purse

In almost every household the same amount of convenience and comfort as housewives enjoy today could be obtained with a good deal less fuel. Less electricity, less gas, and less coal could be used by almost all of us, without any serious difficulty, if we all gave a little more attention to detail. Fuel is not cheap today—especially in the winter—and it is well worth any woman's while to employ her fuel sense and keep more pennies in her purse.

FUEL SENSE

is simply Good Housekeeping

Fuel is money. Every time you turn on a switch or light the gas, and every time you put a lump of coal on the fire you are spending money just as surely as when you hand it over the counter of a shop.

While shopping you try to see that you get value for every penny you spend. You ask yourself questions. You wonder: " Is it worth it ? Couldn't I manage without ? " It is quite easy—once you've got into the way of it--to do just the same thing when you are spending fuel.

Suppose, just for example, that we are thinking of switching on the electric oven to roast the joint. We know that ovens simply gallop away with our electricity-pennies. So we use our fuel sense and say that if we really must spend all those pennies we had better get full value for them. What else can be cooked while the oven's hot ? Roast or baked potatoes

—of course. Yorkshire pudding—if it is beef this week. A pie? Baked apples? Perhaps we could braise some onions, or celery, or parsnips?

All the time the oven is on we should be thinking of those pennies we are spending—a penny every five minutes in some districts. When we remember them, we remember, too, that electric ovens stay really hot for a long time after they are switched off. So twenty minutes or a quarter of an hour before dinner time—just when we are beginning to think about laying the table and making the gravy—our fuel sense tells us to switch off the oven.

And at the very end—if we have a really big fuel sense—we remember the washing-up. When we have taken out the meat, we put a bowl of water in the oven. There'll still be enough heat to warm it up while we carve and eat the dinner!

Of course, this is elementary fuel sense. You probably do it already. Probably your mother taught you. But many of us forget. We forget because we do not keep on telling ourselves that fuel is money.

FUEL SENSE

means these three things

There are three big divisions of fuel sense, and all the hints and tips in this booklet come under one or another of them. They are :

1 *Using the most efficient appliances.*

2 *Making sure that the appliances we have are as efficient as possible.*

3 *Keeping heat in the house (and cold outside) by insulation, draught-prevention and lagging.*

These are essentials. There's no joy in saving 2d. worth of oven-heat when you could have saved 6d. (and had much more tender meat) by pot-roasting on top of the cooker.

There's no fun and no fuel sense in frying on an electric cooker with a pan that does not make proper contact with the hot-plate.

And, of course, it is simply throwing fuel-pennies to the four winds if all our efforts to keep the house warm are frustrated because a big part of the heat escapes through unused chimneys or non-insulated ceilings, while cold draughts come in through the floorboards, under the doors, or round the windows.

FUEL SENSE

says "First things First"

The first thing to do, then, is to look at our appliances. Are they efficient? Can they be improved? Could we buy (or persuade the landlord to put in) something more sensible and—in all probability—more convenient?

Then we must find out how to make the best use of what we've got. This little book is brim-full of really valuable ideas about this.

And we really *must* make sure that we are not simply pouring away our fuel-pennies because our hot-water pipes are not lagged, or because our rooms are draughty, and our attics badly insulated.

Electricity - pennies
should be saved in Danger Hours

In the winter months—and *on the cooler days of English summer*—*it is still very important to use our current by the clock. Every* 1d. *worth of electricity that we can save between* 8 *in the morning and midday and between* 4 *and* 5.30 *in the afternoon is worth a good deal more money to British industry.*

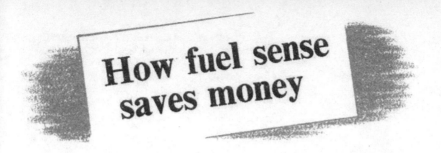

How fuel sense saves money

Cooking with Gas

1 Be careful when using boiling rings—added together they account for about three quarters of the gas used in this country for cooking.

2 Use the smaller ring for all but the largest saucepans. It takes only a little longer to bring them to the boil and saves a lot of gas.

3 Keep the flame under the kettle or saucepan. When it comes up and licks the sides it wastes a lot—and makes pans and kettles dirty, too. A finned-base kettle saves both gas and time.

4 As soon as what you are cooking boils—down with the gas! Quite a small flame keeps things simmering or on the boil.

5 With a *gas* cooker it is more economical to fry than to grill.

6 When using the oven, make it really earn its keep by cooking pies, roasts and cakes at one session.

7 Make full use of the oven-control or thermostat if you have one.

8 If yours is a cooker with a pilot light, keep it turned off at night and when you are not cooking.

9 When grilling or toasting use the heat on top of the grill.

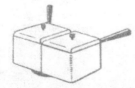

Cooking with Electricity

1 Always switch off the oven and hotplates *before* you have finished cooking. Take fullest advan-

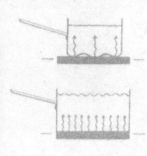

tage of one of the cooker's main features—its thrifty way of storing up heat for you.

2 Two saucepans (particularly square ones) will almost completely cover one boiling plate, and they will boil as quickly as if you used two plates. Three or even four pans can simmer on one plate.

3 On boiling plates use utensils with flat bases and you'll save half your cooking time. That's big money saving!

4 With an *electric* cooker it is more economical to grill than to fry.

5 When grilling, use the top of the grill to heat a saucepan.

6 An electric kettle uses only about half as much current as a boiling plate, so boil water in it for cooking and then pour into the saucepans as required. For most cooking—but *never* for tea—you can fill the kettle from the hot tap and save time.

7 When using the oven for a pudding, cook the vegetables in a casserole in the oven, too, so saving current and dish-washing.

8 When no thermostat is fitted do remember to switch " low " when the oven is hot enough.

Cooking—with Solid Fuel

COMBINATION GRATES

1 Most people who cook with solid fuel have a combination grate. In one of the commonest the oven is beside the fire ; in another it is directly over the fire. The illustration shows a side-oven type, but most of the controls shown in it will be found fitted to the other types, and nearly all the hints apply also to them.

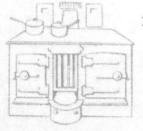

2 Damper Drill. Closing the chimney damper (or pushing in the canopy over the fire) *reduces* the draught to the open fire and *increases* the draught to the oven flue. For cooking, half open the oven flue damper and close the hot-water damper.

For water heating, half open the boiler flue damper and close the one on the oven flue.

3 **Air Supply to Fire.** Most grates have a fret (like a sliding door) under the fire. Except when drawing up the fire just after lighting, keep this fret closed.

4 **Small Coal**—no bigger than walnuts—is best for both cooking and water heating, and slack on top of the fire prevents cold air from entering the flues.

5 **Flues** soon slow up everything and waste a lot of fuel if they are not cleaned regularly every week.

6 **Fuel Sense again!** Allow plenty of time, if you can, for the oven or water to become hot. When the dampers are wide open they use twice as much fuel as when they are half closed. Big savings can be made by fitting a fire brick on the blank side of the grate. Be careful, though! It must not cover the opening of a flue.

Cooking? Season it with Fuel Sense

1 What about a steamer? With one of those two- or three-storied affairs and a spot of thoughtful planning you can cook a whole meal (say, a meat pudding, vegetables, and hot sweet) over a single burner or ring. Tastes better, too!

2 Of course, *you* always keep lids on saucepans when boiling vegetables, soup and stock, boiled puddings, fish, etc. Yet quite a lot of people forget!

3 Shredding or slicing vegetables helps you cook them quickly in very little water. Peas and carrots, or any root vegetables (including potatoes) can be cooked in one saucepan.

4 It is wise to avoid heating a drop more water than you must—and this applies not only to cooking, but to dish washing, clothes, and the weekly wash. Watch that cup of tea : you don't need a kettleful for that!

5 It's a messy job, but it does pay to give burners and hotplates a frequent going-over to remove every trace of grease and burnt food.

6 Utensils are always kept clean inside, but many people don't realise that dirt or soot on the outside slows up cooking and wastes fuel. But you don't want a shiny base. Dull or black ones transfer heat more quickly to what you're cooking.

7 Cooking isn't the household's biggest consumer of electricity or gas, but it gives some of the best opportunities for using fuel sense and saving money.

Hot Water

1 Most water companies will correct dripping taps at short notice, either free or for a nominal charge. (A drip every second can waste a hundredweight of coal a year!)

2 Using two or three inches less water in the bath is no hardship to anyone, but you'd be surprised at the money saved.

3 It is always better to wash-up in a bowl. Most sinks hold too much water ; and they cool it very quickly, too. We have all been guilty at times, but washing hands or dishes under the running tap is shockingly wasteful. Let's try to avoid it.

4 Wash-boilers can safely be turned down as soon as boiling-point is reached.

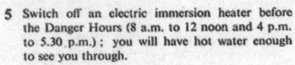

5 Switch off an electric immersion heater before the Danger Hours (8 a.m. to 12 noon and 4 p.m. to 5.30 p.m.) ; you will have hot water enough to see you through.

6 See that all hot water tanks and pipes are properly lagged.

Lighting and Radio

1 Use good lamps or mantles and light-coloured shades, and keep lamps and reflectors bright and shining.

2 In passages and halls and for reading-lamps you seldom need a very bright light.

3   Turning off lamps—and radio sets, too—when you leave a room should be a matter of habit. Two hours' waste of your radio every day uses up half a hundredweight of coal a year at the power station.

Housewarming

1   Turn on fires and radiators only when absolutely necessary—and turn them off at least half an hour before you finally leave the room.

2   Turn on electric or gas fires full only to *heat* the room. Half the fire will *keep* it warm.

3   Even if you will be out of the room only for a few moments, do remember to turn off the fire. After all, you may easily be interrupted and not return for a long time.

4   With old-fashioned open fires, a firebrick at back and sides can easily save a lot of fuel.

5   Start fires with good coal, but keep them going or bank them down with slack or with briquettes. The Ministry of Fuel and Power has an interesting leaflet on making briquettes from coal dust and cement or clay ; why not ask for it ?

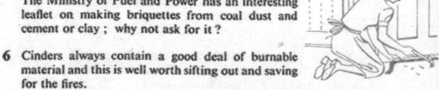

6   Cinders always contain a good deal of burnable material and this is well worth sifting out and saving for the fires.

7   Keep out draughts! (See section on INSULATION.)

Refrigerators

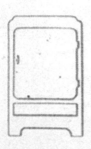

1   Open the door as seldom as you can.

2   Let hot foods cool before they go into the refrigerator.

3   Use it only for perishable foods.

4   Set the temperature control at a low number.

Ironing

1 Electric irons should be switched off for a few minutes from time to time to make use of the stored heat.

2 To heat up an electric iron for one or two small articles is a most expensive habit. " Iron a lot while the iron's hot" is the rule.

Gas Pokers

1 They are handy but they are gluttons for gas. If you lay the fire carefully, using wood when you can get it, you need not use gas pokers for more then five minutes.

Lagging

1 Lagging is BASIC fuel sense, because it can be done very cheaply or without cost at all, and once it's done it stays done, saving fuel and money year after year without trouble or fuss.

2 You can buy ready-made jackets for hot-water tanks or suitable materials specially prepared for lagging. These can be obtained from most ironmongers, builders' merchants, and general stores.

3 At no cost at all you can improvise suitable material from (a) strips of old felt, (b) old carpets, (c) old blankets or quilts, (d) corrugated cardboard or (e) sawdust.

4 Remember that lagging should fit closely and—most important—that it should go on top of the tank as well as round the sides.

5 Hot-water pipes, both flow and return, between the boiler and cylinder or tank should be lagged, too.

6 The Ministry of Fuel and Power has a very interesting leaflet with pictures and diagrams called " LAG AND RELAX." Ask for it!

7 It is a mistake to think that lagging hot-water tanks makes them useless for airing. Sufficient heat will still be available for airing purposes.

"Keep the warmth indoors"

1 You can have warm rooms with less fuel by letting much less heat escape through roofs, chimneys, and windows.

2 Badly fitting doors and windows can be made draught-proof by tacking strips of felt or rubber beading round the edges to seal the cracks.

3 Floors should be fully covered with linoleum or carpet, with an underlayer of newspaper and/or felt. Cracks in floorboards can be caulked with plastic wood from the ironmonger. The gap between floorboards and skirting should also be sealed.

4 When fires are not used the flue or chimney should be blocked.

5 Heat rises. It escapes up stairs and through the ceiling into the attic. It can be stopped by laying insulation on the attic floor or between the joists. Ask the Ministry of Fuel and Power for the illustrated leaflet on "Attic Insulation."

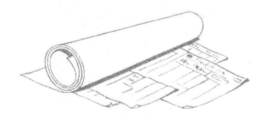

How much does it use?

Some gas and electrical appliances have much bigger appetites for fuel—and money—than others. Here's a guide that shows you which are the greedy ones, so you can be extra careful not to use them for a second longer than you must.

ELECTRICAL EQUIPMENT

APPLIANCE	USES ONE UNIT IN
Immersion heater	¼ hour
Wash boiler	20 minutes
Sink storage heater	½ hour
Oven (on full)	40 minutes
Grill (on full)	½ to 1 hour
Boiling plate (on full)	½ to 1 hour
Fire (two bars)	½ hour
Fire (one bar)	1 hour
Kettle	1 hour
Toaster	2 hours
Electric iron	2 to 3 hours
Vacuum cleaner	6 hours
100-watt lamp	10 hours
60-watt lamp	16 hours
Radio	20 hours
Refrigerator	1 day
Electric clock	1,000 hours

GAS EQUIPMENT

APPLIANCE	CUBIC FEET PER HOUR
Multi-point heater	180
Bath geyser	150
Sink water heater (on full)	75
Wash boiler (on full)	40
Medium fire (on full)	30
Poker (on full)	25
Grill (on full)	25
Large ring (on full)	25
Oven (on full)	22
(average use)	10
Small ring (on full)	15
Ordinary gas light	5
Gas iron	5
Refrigerator	1

ISSUED BY THE MINISTRY OF FUEL AND POWER

Printed for H.M. Stationery Office by Fosh & Cross Ltd., London. 51-120

HEAT PLAYS
HAVOC
WITH SHOE
LEATHER

Your boots and shoes have now got to last you far longer than they ever did before, as leather and rubber are vitally needed for the Fighting Services. This leaflet contains hints to help you to get more wear out of your footwear—with additional hints overleaf about the care of stockings.

The first point to remember is that any strong heat ruins wet shoes, so don't dry yours close to the fire or on a radiator. When you sit by the fireside don't have your feet close to the fire.

Change from your outdoor shoes into slippers or an old pair of shoes to reduce wear and tear on your serviceable footwear.

REGULAR CLEANING AND POLISHING

not only improve the looks but lengthen the life of your shoes. First remove dirt and dust, then rub very little polish well in to feed the leather and keep it pliable. Always apply polish when shoes are to be put away for a time.

Suede shoes should be brushed after each wearing but not while they are still wet.

For heavy leather boots use dubbin, which preserves the leather and keeps it waterproof, but it will remove the shine.

If you have two pairs of shoes wear them on alternate days. They last much longer this way as the "day off" gives the leather time to dry out thoroughly.

If you have no shoe trees for keeping your shoes in shape, stuff the shoes well with paper, but remember not to put shoe trees in *wet* shoes or they may stretch.

Perspiration ruins boots and shoes. Before going out in hot weather sprinkle dusting powder sparingly inside stockings and socks or inside the shoes themselves if stockings are not being worn, take off your shoes as soon as you get home and bathe your feet in cold water.

NEVER TRY TO FORCE YOUR FEET

into a pair of laced shoes that have not been loosened sufficiently or you will do permanent damage to the stiff backs of the shoes, and never take them off without undoing them. See that the children don't get into this bad habit.

Watch how your shoes are wearing. It is a mistake to go on wearing shoes until they no longer protect your feet in wet weather. Badly worn heels will soon spoil shoes and throw them out of balance. Have them built up directly the first layer of leather is worn down.

WHEN YOUR BOOTS & SHOES NEED REPAIRING *take the advice of your shoe repairer; he will know what to do for the best and what repairs he is allowed to do.*

WOODEN - SOLED SHOES

should never be allowed to wear down to the wooden sole as this cannot be replaced. Have the leather bars attended to in good time.

Wear new or newly repaired shoes for the first time on a dry day, never on a wet day. Little particles of grit will work their way into the surface of the leather sole and act as a reinforcement.

RUBBER BOOTS AND WELLINGTONS are very precious,

so only wear *them to keep out the wet,*

and see that the children keep their gumboots for really wet days and never let them wear them for any other purpose.

Clean rubber boots with a wet cloth and plain water—never use soap—and dry thoroughly by wiping—never put them near heat.

Put them away in a dark, dry place. Don't let them be folded or bent. Wellingtons with soft tops should be stuffed with paper to prevent them bending.

SOCKS. Woollen socks should be

bought large enough to allow for shrinking. When knitting socks work in a strong cotton thread with the wool at the heels and toes.

Mend any hole or thin place as soon as it appears. Many large holes in the heels of socks can be mended either by being darned over a scrap of net or by patching with a piece of new knitting—or a piece from an old sock.

Perspiration tends to rot socks so they should be rinsed frequently, and —never boil socks or stockings.

WHY NOT EXCHANGE CHILDREN'S OUT-GROWN SHOES?

In countless cupboards throughout the country, children's shoes are lying idle, not because they are outworn, but because they are out-grown. Perhaps the local school, welfare clinic, or some local women's organisation may already be running a children's shoe exchange—or be planning to run one. It's worth finding out, anyhow.

STOCKINGS. If you really need

to buy new stockings be sure to get the right size. When buying non-fully fashioned stockings you will probably need a size larger than with fully fashioned stockings. Reinforce the heels and toes by darning. Oversew the centre seam at the heel on the inside and rinse the stockings through in warm water before wearing them. A

patch the size of a penny herring-boned in position at the top of stockings (see illustration) makes a strong reinforcement for the suspender grips. Re-foot women's rayon, lisle, cotton and wool stockings by cutting the new foot from the good parts of the discarded stocking, turning in the edges and sewing firmly in place on top of the worn foot with a fine needle. When putting on your stockings turn in the toe and gently roll the stocking over the foot and up the leg. Take care that rings and finger nails don't catch the threads. Don't suspend stockings too tightly; and if they are too short, add a piece at the top, from an old stocking to lengthen (see sketch).

WASHING HINTS. *Rayon stockings should always be rinsed before they are put on for the first time, and if possible every time you take them off. They should be handled gently when wet, and when washing don't rub or wring them, squeeze gently in soapy water, rinse out thoroughly and be sure they are bone dry before putting them on.*